STEVE AND MEGUMI BIDDLE'S

THE NEW
ORIGAMI

STEVE AND MEGUMI BIDDLE'S
THE NEW ORIGAMI

With illustrations by Megumi Biddle

BCA

LONDON   NEW YORK   SYDNEY   TORONTO

First Published 1993

1 3 5 7 9 10 8 6 4 2

DESIGNER: Terry Jeavons

This edition published 1993 by BCA by arrangement with
Ebury Press Limited, Random House, 20 Vauxhall Bridge Road,
London SW1V 2SA

CN 4515

A CIP catalogue record for this book is available from
the British Library

Printed in Great Britain by Butler & Tanner, Frome and London

Papers used by Ebury Press are natural recyclable products
made from wood grown in sustainable forests.

CONTENTS

INTRODUCTION

Origami has become an international art. Every year the world of origami grows bigger; its popularity has grown not only in Japan but worldwide. The word 'origami' is now understood in any country in the world, and many people from many different countries practise it, many of them creating their own original models and exchanging ideas with other enthusiasts worldwide.

Anyone can enjoy origami, regardless of age, sex, nationality and language. Its characteristics are instrumental in stimulating and enriching the imagination, encouraging creative ideas and a geometrical way of thinking. Consequently, it has come to be adopted as teaching material in Japan and many other countries. Origami is also effective in the medical world as a means of rehabilitation, and it makes a very good pastime for those enjoying their retirement.

If you have never tried origami before, *New Origami* is a good book to begin with. It will introduce you to some traditional origami folds as well as to many new ones. If you are already accomplished at origami, we hope that you will be excited by the new folds in this book (many of them featured for the first time) and the various ways in which they can be used.

This book has been designed to take you, the folder, from the very first, easy steps, to the much more intricate methods used to produce many original designs. By all means, aim to copy the models exactly as they appear in the diagrams at first, but what is important is your own personal touch and how you develop the ideas.

You may be wondering what sort of paper to use for the origami projects. Most of the models in this book are folded from a single square of paper, although in a few cases you will need more than just one, or you will need a rectangular piece of paper. All kinds of paper can be folded into origami, but try to find a type that suits you best. Packets of origami paper, coloured on one side and white on the other, can be obtained from department stores, art and craft shops, toy shops, stationery shops and oriental gift shops. However, any type of paper (as long as it folds well) is suitable for origami. Why not try using fancy gift wrapping paper, or you could even cut a few pages out of a colour magazine! Your paper does not have to be coloured on one side, but it can help some origami models look very attractive and can make some of the illustrations easier to follow.

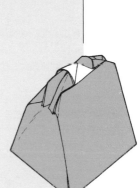

If you want to learn more about origami, contact the British Origami Society, 11 Yarningale Road, Kings Heath, Birmingham, B14 6LT, or, in the United States, contact the Friends of the Origami Center of America, 15 West 77th Street, New York, NY 10024-5192.

We would very much like to hear from you about your interest in origami, or if you have any problems in obtaining origami materials, so please write to us, care of our publishers (see page 4), enclosing a stamped addressed envelope.

Finally, we would like to echo the words of our many origami friends: always remember that the real secret of origami lies in the giving and sharing with others. We do hope you have a lot of fun in discovering the creative possibilities of origami.

STEVE AND MEGUMI BIDDLE

The Authors

Steve Biddle is a professional entertainer with a speciality act that has taken him all over the world. He studied origami in Japan with the top Japanese origami masters, thereby acquiring deeper knowledge of a subject that has always fascinated him. Megumi is a highly qualified graphic artist, designer and illustrator, with a long-standing interest in paper and its many applications. The superb illustrations in this book are also her own.

Steve and Megumi combine their talents to design items for television, feature films and major advertising campaigns, and in writing books for children and adults. They have appeared on many prestigious television programmes and currently present a weekly origami programme for Sky TV.

Acknowledgements
Our deepest thanks go to our many paper folding friends who have given permission for their models to be included in this book.

HELPFUL TIPS

Before you try any of the procedures or projects in this book, here are some very helpful tips that will make origami easier:

● Try to obtain the kind of paper most suitable for the origami you plan to fold, as this will help enhance the finished model.

● Before you start, make sure your paper is the correct shape.

● Fold on a smooth flat surface, such as a table or book.

● Make your folds neat and accurate.

● Press your folds into place by running your thumb nail along them.

● Do not panic if your first few attempts at folding are not very successful. With practice you will come to understand the many ways in which a piece of paper behaves when it is folded.

● In the diagrams in this book, the shading represents the coloured side of the paper.

● Look at each diagram carefully, read the instructions, then look ahead to the next diagram to see what shape should be created when you have completed the step you are working on.

● You will find it easiest to work your way through from the beginning of this book to the end, as some of the folding projects and procedures in later sections are based partially on previous ones. However, if you are an experienced paperfolder and can follow origami instructions without too much help, you can, of course, select any design as a starting point.

● Above all, if a fold or a whole model does not work out, do not give up hope. Go through all the illustrations one by one, checking that you have read the instructions correctly and have not missed an important word or overlooked a symbol. If you are still unable to complete the model, put it to one side and come back to it another day with a fresh mind.

SYMBOLS AND BASIC FOLDING PROCEDURES

The symbols used in this book have been developed by the Nippon Origami Association, and it is important that you understand them as they show you the direction in which the paper should be folded. Look very carefully at the diagrams to see which way the dashes, dots and arrows go over, through and under, and fold your paper accordingly.

If you are new to origami and are folding for the first time, you may be worried about understanding all the paperfolding jargon. If this is the case, we suggest that, before trying any of the origami projects, you take a few squares of paper and study the following symbols and folding procedures. In this way, you will get to know the most basic points about origami. After spending a few minutes learning them, you will be able to fold from almost any book on origami, even if you cannot understand the language in which it is written.

VALLEY FOLD

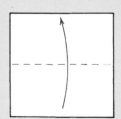

1 This is the simplest and most common technique to be found in origami. A valley fold (fold forwards or in front) is shown by a line of dashes and a solid arrow showing the direction in which the paper has to be folded.

2 To make a valley fold, hold down the top edge of a square of paper. Lift the bottom edge . . .

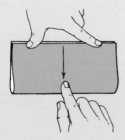

3 and bring it up to meet the top edge. Keeping the edges together, run your forefinger down the middle of the paper to the bottom edge.

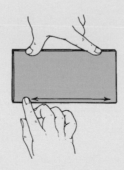

4 Run your forefinger along the bottom edge to both sides, thereby completing the fold. If you turn the paper sideways on and unfold it a little, you can see the shape resembles a valley, hence the name of this fold.

MOUNTAIN FOLD

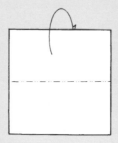

1 A mountain fold (fold backwards or behind) is shown by a line of dots and dashes (usually a long dash followed by two dots) and a hollow-headed arrow. As in the valley fold, the arrow always shows the direction in which the paper has to be folded.

2 To make a mountain fold, hold the bottom edge of a square of paper. Bend the top edge backwards . . .

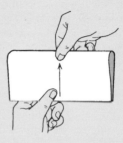

3 and take it down to meet the bottom edge.

4 Keeping the edges together, run your thumb up the middle of the paper to the top edge. Run your thumb and fingers along the top edge, thereby completing the fold. If you turn the paper sideways on and unfold it a little, you can see the shape resembles a mountain, hence the name of this fold.

FOLD AND UNFOLD

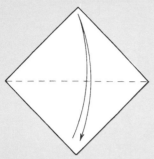

1 An arrow which comes back on itself means 'Fold, press flat and unfold the paper back to its previous position'.

2 Turn a square of paper around to look like a diamond. Valley fold it in half from bottom to top, thereby making a triangle. Press it flat.

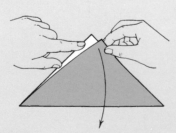

3 Unfold the triangle completely.

4 This is the completed fold and unfold. A faint, solid line represents an existing fold-line, i.e. one that is the result of a previous step.

STEP FOLD

1 A zigzagged arrow drawn on top of the diagram means 'Fold the paper in the direction shown by the arrow'. A step fold is made by pleating the paper in a valley and mountain fold, so it becomes like a step.

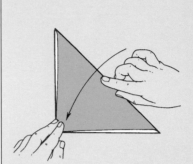

2 To create a step fold, valley fold a square of paper in half from top right to bottom left, thereby making a triangle.

3 From the bottom left-hand corner, valley fold the top layer of paper up, so . . .

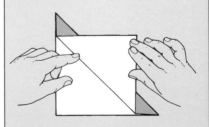

4 it lies over the triangle's longest side. Press it flat, thereby completing the step fold.

TURN OVER

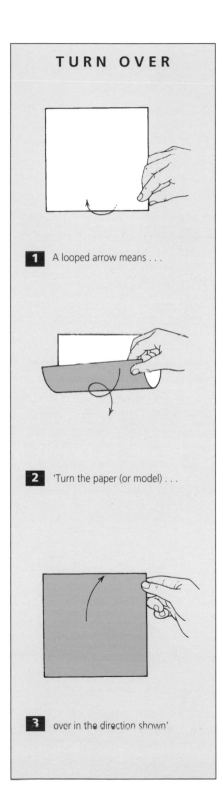

1 A looped arrow means . . .

2 'Turn the paper (or model) . . .

3 over in the direction shown'

TURN AROUND

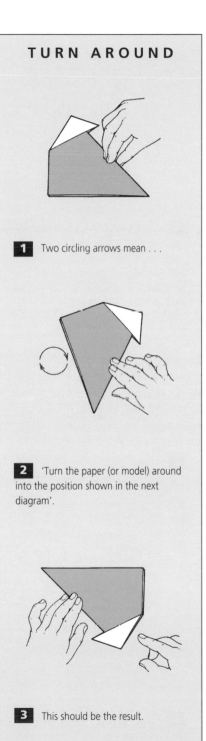

1 Two circling arrows mean . . .

2 'Turn the paper (or model) around into the position shown in the next diagram'.

3 This should be the result.

PULL OUT

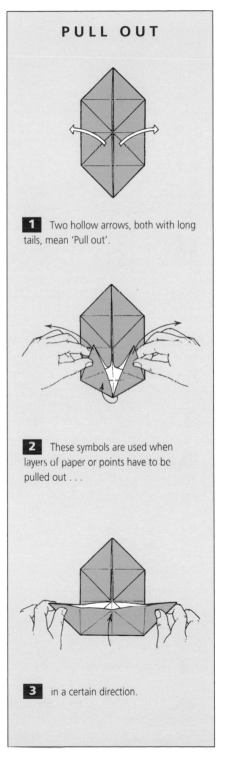

1 Two hollow arrows, both with long tails, mean 'Pull out'.

2 These symbols are used when layers of paper or points have to be pulled out . . .

3 in a certain direction.

INSERT

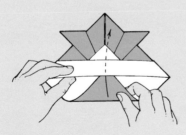

1 A single hollow arrow with a long tail means 'Insert'.

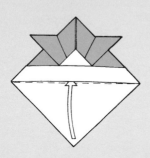

2 This symbol is used when a flap or point has to be inserted either into a pocket . . .

3 or underneath a layer of paper.

INSIDE REVERSE FOLD

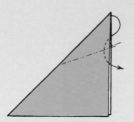

1 Inside reverse folds are very easy to do. After valley and mountain folds, they are the most commonly used technique in origami. An inside reverse fold is indicated by a wavy arrow and a mountain fold-line.

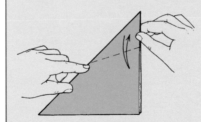

2 To create an inside reverse fold, valley fold a square of paper in half from top left to bottom right, to make a triangle. To prepare for the inside reverse fold, valley fold the top right-hand point of the paper at the required angle. Press it flat and unfold it.

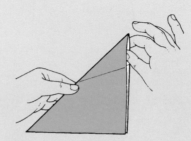

3 Insert your thumb between the right-hand layers of paper and place your forefinger on the triangle's ridge.

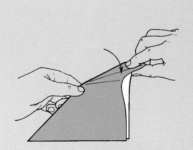

4 Draw back your forefinger, at the same time pushing down on the ridge to change it into a valley fold.

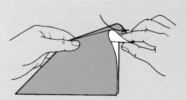

5 Using the fold-lines created in step 2 as a guide, pull the point down inside the model as shown.

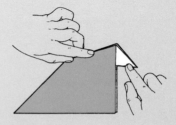

6 Press the paper flat, thereby completing the inside reverse fold. This technique is so named because the paper is folded inside and a ridge is reversed from a mountain to a valley fold.

OUTSIDE REVERSE FOLD

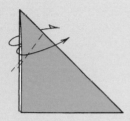

1 An outside reverse fold also requires a little preparation beforehand. This technique is indicated by solid and hollow-headed arrows, and valley and mountain fold-lines.

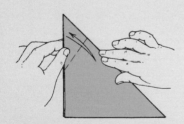

2 To create an outside reverse fold, valley fold a square of paper in half from top right to bottom left, to make a triangle. Valley fold the top left-hand point of the triangle over at the required angle. Press the point flat, then unfold it.

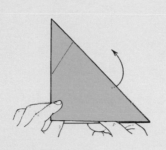

3 Separate the layers of paper, . . .

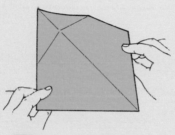

4 taking one to the front and one to the back.

5 Press down on the fold-lines made in step 3, to convert them into valley folds, at the same time . . .

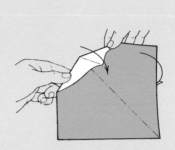

6 bringing the top point forwards.

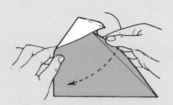

7 Mountain fold the paper in half along the middle fold-line.

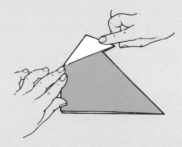

8 Press the paper flat, thereby completing the outside reverse fold. This technique is so named because the paper being folded moves outside the rest of the paper and fold-lines are reversed.

OPEN AND SQUASH

1   The open and squash technique is not at all tricky to do. As open and squash folds can come in many shapes and disguises, it is important to learn this technique carefully. An open and squash is shown by a hollow arrow with a short, indented tail.

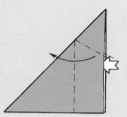

2   Valley fold a square of paper in half from top left to bottom right, to make a triangle. Valley fold the right-hand side of the triangle over towards the left (the exact position of the fold is not important). Press the side flat and unfold it.

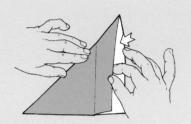

3   Lift the side up along the fold-line that has just been made. Insert your fingers between the layers of paper.

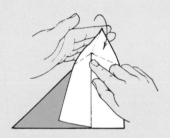

4   Start to open out the layers and, with your other hand, . . .

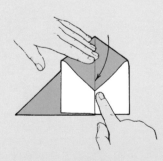

5   squash the point down neatly into this shape. Press the paper flat to complete the open and squash technique, which is so named because layers of paper or a pocket are opened out and squashed down.

ENLARGE

1   A swollen arrow with a pointed tail shows that the following diagram . . .

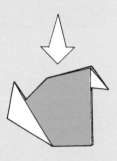

2   is drawn to a larger scale.

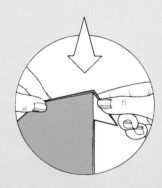

3   To clarify a tricky (or detailed) procedure, an enlargement of it is illustrated inside a circle.

FOLD OVER AND OVER

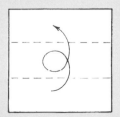

1 A looped arrow drawn on top of a diagram means 'Fold the paper over and over again in the direction shown by the arrow'. Each fold-line represents one fold-over move.

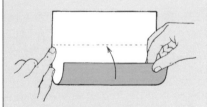

2 Valley fold the bottom edge of a square of paper up to a point that is about one-third of the distance to the top edge.

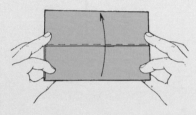

3 Valley fold the bottom 'folded' edge up to meet the top edge.

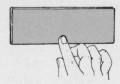

4 Press the paper flat, thereby completing the fold over and over technique.

SINK

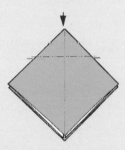

1 This technique involves pushing a point between four layers of paper. A sink is indicated by a solid arrow with a mountain fold-line, or with mountain and valley fold-lines if the sink is to be a multi-sink.

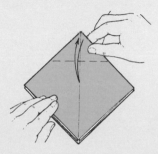

2 The starting point is a preliminary fold (see page 80). First mark the fold-line by folding down the top point in a valley fold. Press it flat and unfold it.

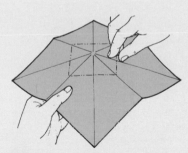

3 Unfold the paper and flatten the central point. Crease the four sides of the inner square into mountain folds, so it looks like a table top.

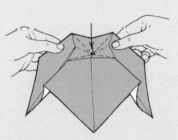

4 Push down on the middle of the square, at the same time pushing in the sides so they collapse towards the middle. Keep on pushing until the square fully collapses, thereby inverting the point inside the model.

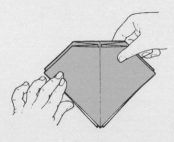

5 Here is the completed sink.

HOW TO MAKE 'A'-SIZED PAPER

In paper manufacturing, paper sizes are classified as A, B or C. A-sized sheets of paper are rectangular in the proportions of 1:1.414. In the United Kingdom, A4 paper is readily available and used for a whole range of printed material. Some of the projects in *New Origami* start with A-sized paper; here are two quick and easy methods to make an A-sized rectangle.

From a Square

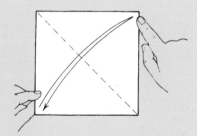

1 Valley fold a square of paper in half from bottom left to top right, thereby making a triangle. Press it flat and unfold it.

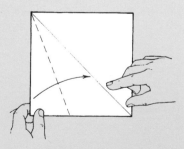

2 Valley fold the left-hand side over to lie against the diagonal fold-line.

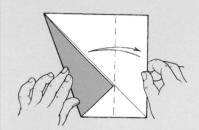

3 Valley fold the right-hand side over along a vertical line as shown. Press it flat and unfold it.

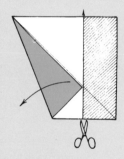

4 Cut along the fold-line made in step 3 and discard the shaded oblong of paper. (The new symbol of a pair of scissors and a solid line means 'Cut the paper'. The solid line shows the position of the cut.) To complete, open out the paper into . . .

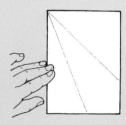

5 an A-sized rectangle.

From a Rectangle

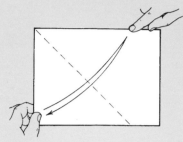

1 Place the rectangle sideways on. Valley fold the left-hand side up to meet the top edge. Press it flat and unfold it.

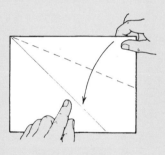

2 Valley fold the top edge over to lie against the diagonal fold-line.

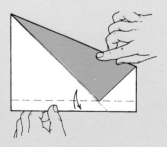

3 Valley fold the bottom edge up along a horizontal line as shown. Press it flat and unfold it.

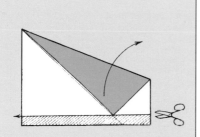

4 Cut along the fold-line made in step 3 and discard the shaded strip of paper. To complete, open out the paper into . . .

5 an A-sized rectangle.

If, in step 2, the top right-hand corner protrudes beyond the bottom edge . . .

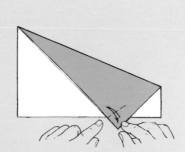

6 valley fold the protruding corner up to where the sloping and bottom edges intersect. Press down on the paper only a little as shown. Unfold it.

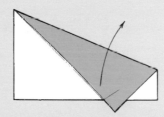

7 Open out the paper.

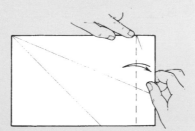

8 Valley fold the right-hand side over along a vertical line, as shown. Press it flat and unfold it.

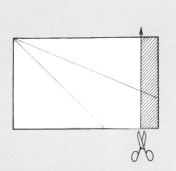

9 Cut along the fold-line made in step 8 and discard the shaded strip of paper . . .

10 to produce an A-sized rectangle.

MODULAR ORIGAMI

Modular origami consists of folding non-representational shapes or units and fitting them together to build more complex constructions. In the hands of an expert, such as Tomoko Fuse, it can be the means of creating decorative boxes using many sheets of paper.

Traditional examples of modular origami, such as the kusudama (see page 26), may be glued together; present-day paperfolders prefer their modular constructions to be held together by interlocking. The models that follow use both techniques.

CUBE

TRADITIONAL

Once this cube has been mastered, it is a very easy item to use as a construction piece when making solid geometrical shapes, such as the soma cube on page 41.

USE SIX SQUARES OF PAPER, IDENTICAL IN SIZE, WHITE SIDE UP.

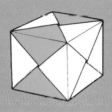

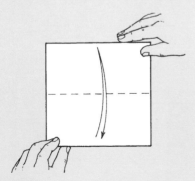

1 Valley fold one square in half from bottom to top. Press it flat and unfold it.

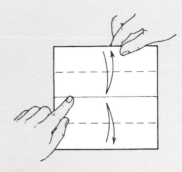

2 Valley fold the top and bottom edges to meet the middle fold-line. Press them flat and unfold them.

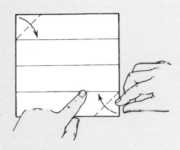

3 Valley fold the top left-hand corner over to meet the adjacent fold-line. Repeat this step with the bottom right-hand corner.

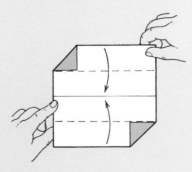

4 Once again, valley fold the top and bottom edges to meet the middle fold-line.

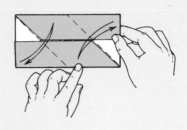

5 Valley fold the right-hand side down, so that it lies along the bottom edge. Valley fold the left-hand side up, so that it lies along the top edge. Press them flat and unfold them.

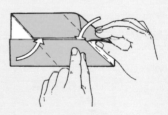

6 Repeat step 5, but tuck the right-hand side underneath the lower layer of paper, and the left-hand side underneath the upper layer of paper, so . . .

7 completing one unit of the cube. Now make five more units in the same way.

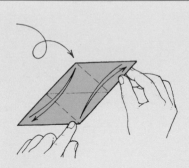

8 Turn all the units over. Valley fold the top right- and bottom left-hand triangular points in as shown. Press them flat and unfold them.

Joining the Units Together

As a help during assembly, label the units from A to F, with a pencil.

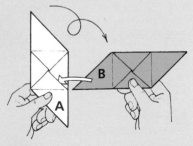

9 Turn all the units over. Tuck unit B into unit A from the right-hand side.

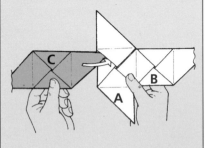

10 Tuck unit C into unit A from the left-hand side.

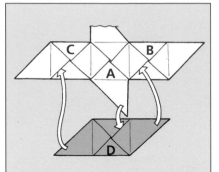

11 Tuck unit A into unit D from above. Tuck unit D into units B and C, so that . . .

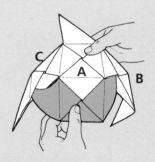

12 the units become three-dimensional.

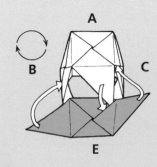

13 Turn the units around. Tuck unit A into unit E. Tuck unit E into units B and C.

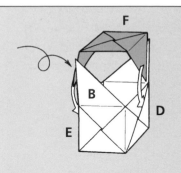

14 Turn the units over. Tuck unit F into units D and E.

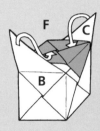

15 Finally, tuck units B and C into unit F, thereby . . .

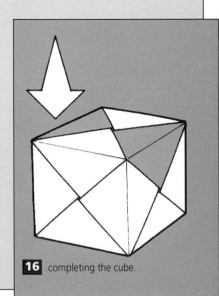

16 completing the cube.

PENTAGON COASTER (DODECAHEDRON)

FRANCIS OW

These models are not difficult to make, but the folding should be as accurate as possible, and you will need patience to produce the necessary number of units.

USE 60 SQUARES OF PAPER, IDENTICAL IN SIZE, WHITE SIDE UP.

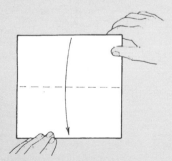

1 Valley fold one square in half from top to bottom, thereby making a shape that in origami is called the book fold.

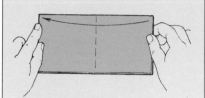

2 Valley fold the book fold in half from side to side, but do not press the paper completely flat.

3 Press down on the paper only a little, at the middle point, then unfold it.

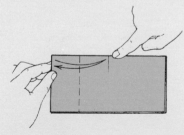

4 Valley fold the left-hand side over to meet the fold-mark made in step 3. Again, do not press the paper flat, but only mark the quarter point. Return the side to its original position.

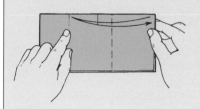

5 Valley fold the right-hand side over to meet the fold-mark made in step 4. Again, do not press the paper flat, but only mark the paper as shown. Return the side to its original position.

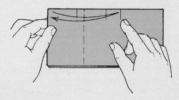

6 Valley fold the left-hand side over the meet the fold-mark made in step 5. Once again, do not press the paper flat, but only mark the paper as shown. Return the side to its original position.

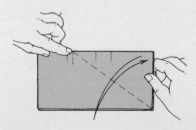

7 Valley fold the top edge down on a line between the fold-mark made in step 6 and the bottom right-hand corner. Press it flat and unfold it.

8 Along the fold-lines made in step 7, inside reverse fold the top edge, thereby . . .

9 completing one unit. Now make 59 more units in the same way.

Joining the Units Together

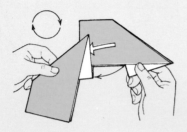

10 Take five units and tuck one unit inside another as shown.

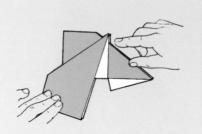

11 This should be the result.

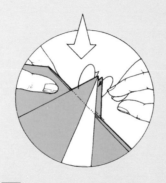

12 Mountain fold the top unit's triangular points down inside the adjoining unit, thereby locking them both together.

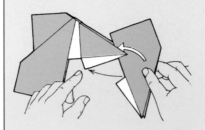

13 Continue tucking and locking the five units together carefully, until . . .

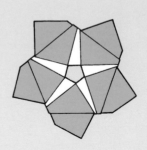

14 you have built up this pentagon coaster design.

Dodecahedron Assembly

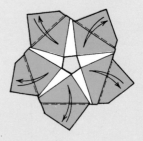

15 Repeat steps 10 to 14 with the remaining 55 units, thereby making a further 11 pentagon coasters. Valley fold one pentagon coaster's flaps over as shown. Press them flat and unfold them. Repeat on all the other coasters.

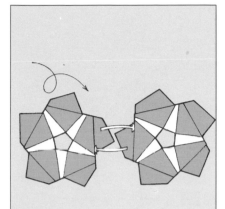

16 Turn all the coasters over. Take two coasters and tuck them together as shown.

17 When a third coaster is tucked into place, . . .

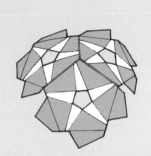

18 the form of the final structure will start to emerge. Make a total of four triple-module units by joining the others in the same way.

19 Link three triple-module units by tucking flaps into pockets.

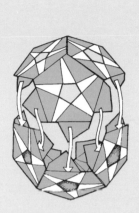

20 Add the remaining unit, thereby . . .

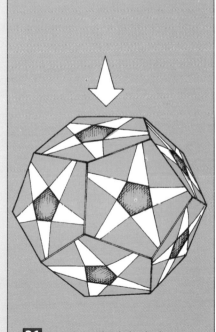

21 completing the dodecahedron.

SIX-PIECE HARLEQUIN STAR

FRANCIS OW

Made out of shiny metallic gift paper, this star would make an ideal Christmas decoration.

USE SIX SQUARES OF PAPER, IDENTICAL IN SIZE, THREE WHITE SIDE UP, AND THREE COLOURED SIDE UP.

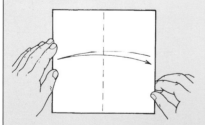

1 Valley fold one square in half from side to side. Press it flat and unfold it.

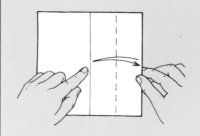

2 Valley fold the right-hand side over to meet the middle fold-line. Do not press the paper flat, but only mark the quarter point. Return the side to its original position.

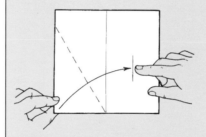

3 Starting in the middle of the bottom edge, valley fold the bottom left-hand corner over to meet the fold-mark made in step 2.

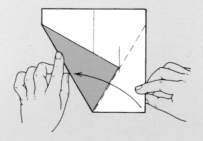

4 Valley fold the bottom right-hand corner over, so that it lies on top, . . .

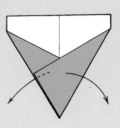

5 as shown. Unfold the paper completely.

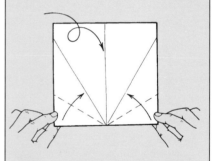

6 Turn the paper over. Valley fold the bottom left-hand edge over to meet the adjacent fold-line as shown. Repeat this step with the bottom right-hand edge.

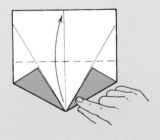

7 Valley fold the paper in half from bottom to top.

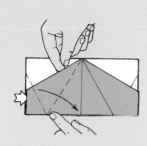

8 Using the existing fold-lines as a guide, valley fold the left-hand sloping edge over to lie along the middle fold-line, at the same time . . .

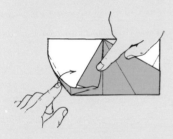

9 opening out and squashing the lower left-hand corner.

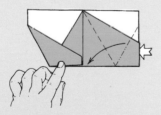

10 This should be the result. Repeat steps 8 and 9 with the right-hand sloping edge, thereby making a triangular point.

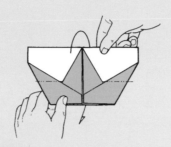

11 Mountain fold the top edge behind on a line where the sloping edges and the triangular point's sides intersect.

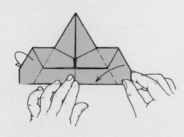

12 Valley fold the right-hand flap of paper over the point's adjacent side. Mountain fold the left-hand flap of paper behind as shown, thereby . . .

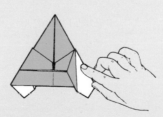

13 completing one unit of the harlequin star. Now make five more such units.

Joining the Units Together

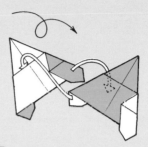

14 Turn all the units over. Tuck a white unit and a coloured unit together as shown, thereby locking them together.

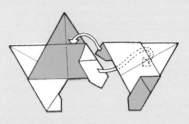

15 Working around in a clockwise direction and alternating between white and coloured units, continue tucking and locking units together carefully, . . .

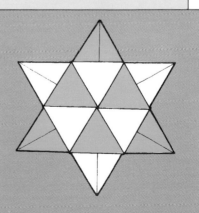

16 until you have built up a six-piece harlequin star design.

KUSUDAMA

(TRADITIONAL)
INTRODUCED BY
MEGUMI BIDDLE

In pre-modern Japan (about AD 500 to 600), it was the custom on 5 May to collect iris flowers and to sew them around a pot-pourri of herbs. This sweet-smelling decoration (kusudama) was then given as a gift, signifying the wishes of the giver that the receiver should enjoy good health. Nowadays, the kusudama is made from paper or origami flowers, 5 May is celebrated as Children's Day, and the wishes of good health are passed on to children.

USE 60 SQUARES OF PAPER, IDENTICAL IN SIZE, WHITE SIDE UP.
YOU WILL ALSO NEED A TUBE OF PAPER GLUE.

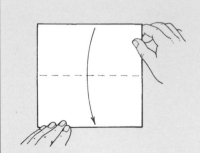

1   Valley fold one square in half from top to bottom.

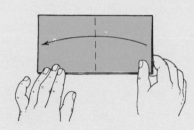

2   Valley fold the book fold in half from right to left.

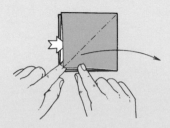

3   Lift the top left-hand layer up along the middle fold-line.
Open out the paper and, with your free hand, . . .

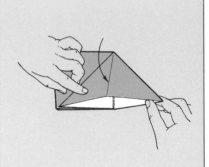

4   squash it down neatly into a triangle.

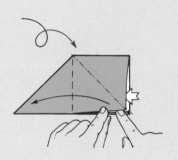

5   Turn the paper over. Repeat step 3 with the top right-hand layer of paper.

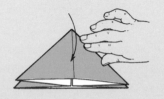

6   Repeat step 4, thereby making a shape that in origami is called the waterbomb base.

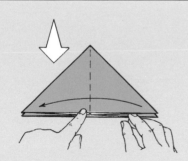

7 Valley fold the top right-hand flap of paper over to the left, like turning the page of a book.

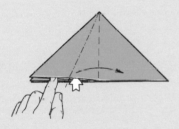

8 Open out the top left-hand flap and squash it down neatly into the position shown in step 9.

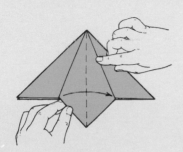

9 Valley fold the squashed flap in half from left to right.

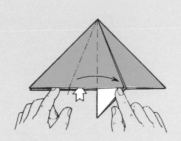

10 Repeat steps 8 and 9 with the remaining two left-hand flaps. But do *not* valley fold the last squashed flap in half, instead . . .

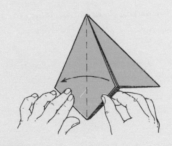

11 valley fold *all* the squashed flaps in half from right to left.

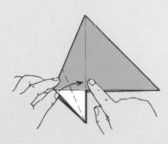

12 Valley fold the front flap's lower sloping edge over, so that it lies along the vertical fold line.

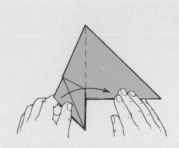

13 Valley fold two left-hand flaps over towards the right.

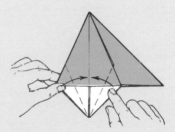

14 Valley fold the front *flap's* lower sloping edges over, so they lie along the vertical fold-line.

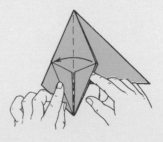

15 Valley fold the top right-hand flap over to the left.

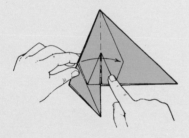

16 Valley fold the front point up as far as it will go.

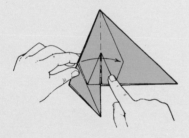

17 Valley fold three left-hand flaps over towards the right. Repeat steps 14, 15 and 16 with the front flap.

18 Valley fold three left-hand flaps over towards the right. Repeat steps 12, 15 and 16. Press the paper flat.

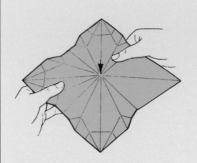

19 Unfold the paper completely. Press down on the paper's middle with the coloured side on top, thereby making it become bowl-like in appearance.

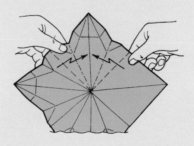

20 Position the paper as shown. Starting with the top point and using the existing fold-lines, step fold the middle of the top right and left edges behind to the middle.

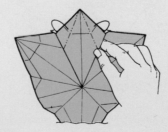

21 Mountain fold the sloping sides behind.

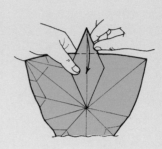

22 Valley fold the top point down along the line of the horizontal edge.

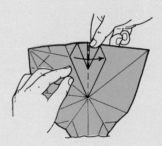

23 Valley fold the inner section of paper in half from left to right.

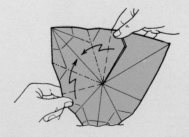

24 Step fold the middle of the left-hand point's two edges behind, in effect repeating step 20. Now repeat steps 21, 22 and 23.

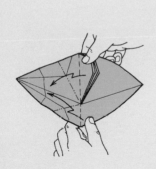

25 Repeat steps 20 and 21 with what was originally the bottom point.

26 Tuck the point down into the model along the line of the horizontal edge, thereby . . .

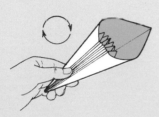

27 completing one petal. Repeat steps 1 to 26 with the remaining 59 squares.

Joining the Units Together

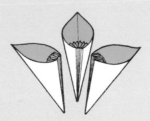

28 Glue five petal units together by means of their vertical edges as shown, thereby . . .

29 making one flower. Repeat step 28, thereby making a further 11 flowers.

30 Glue five flowers into a ring by the tips of their petals as shown. Next, glue another flower into the middle of the ring, thereby completing one half of the kusudama.

31 Make the other half by repeating step 30 with the remaining six flowers. Glue the two halves of the kusudama together as shown.

32 Here is the completed kusudama.

DECORATIVE BOX

TOMOKO FUSE

For a creative challenge, try folding the following units in a variety of colours and joining them together in a different way from the one illustrated.

USE EIGHT SQUARES OF PAPER, IDENTICAL IN SIZE, WHITE SIDE UP.

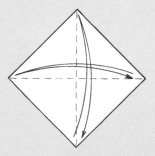

Lid

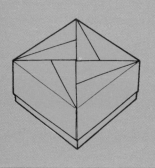

1 Turn one square around to look like a diamond. Valley fold the opposite corners together in turn to mark the diagonal fold-lines, then open up again.

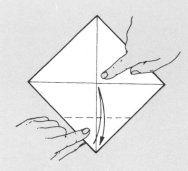

2 Valley fold the bottom corner into the middle. Do not press the paper completely flat, but just press down on it a little. Return the corner to its original position.

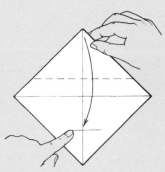

3 Valley fold the top corner down to meet the fold-mark made in step 2, thereby making a coloured triangle.

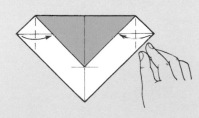

4 Valley fold the right- and left-hand corners in as shown.

5 Unfold the coloured triangle.

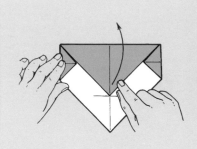

6 Valley fold the paper in half from bottom to top.

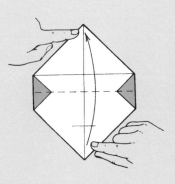

7 Valley fold the bottom edge up to meet the fold-mark made in step 2. Press it flat and unfold it.

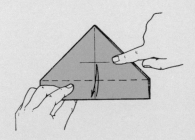

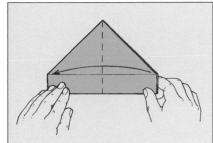

8 Valley fold the paper in half from right to left.

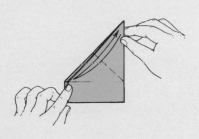

9 Valley fold the right-hand side down to lie along the horizontal fold-line as shown, thereby making a triangle. Press it flat and unfold it.

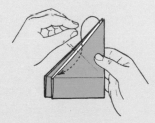

10 Using the fold-lines made in step 9 as a guide, inside reverse fold the inner layer of paper down inside the model as shown, thereby making an inner flap.

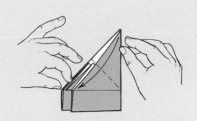

11 Repeat step 9, but do not unfold the triangle.

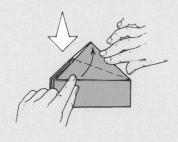

12 Valley fold the triangle's bottom edge over to lie along the right-hand sloping side, thereby making a small triangle.

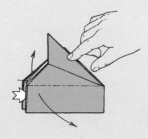

13 Separate the front layer from the back layer, so the model becomes three-dimensional.

14 Valley fold the inner flap across to the other side so that it lies underneath the small triangle, as shown, thereby completing one unit of the lid. Now make three more units in the same way.

Joining the Units Together

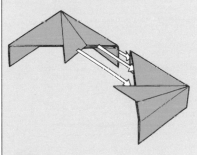

15 Insert one unit deep into the side pocket of another, thereby tucking its inner flap (see steps 10 and 14) between the pocket's sloping layers, at the same time arranging its small triangle (see step 12) to fit under the other unit's small triangle, as shown.

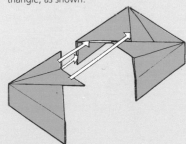

16 Repeat step 15 with the remaining units.

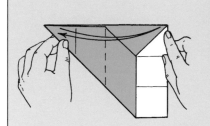

20 Valley fold the top right-hand corner over to meet the adjacent fold-line. Repeat with the bottom left-hand corner.

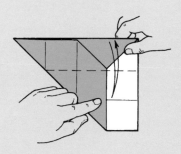

23 Valley fold the paper in half from right to left. Press it flat and unfold it.

17 Here is the completed lid.

Base

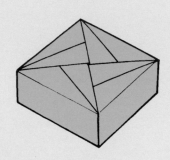

18 Valley fold one square in half from bottom to top. Press it flat and unfold it.

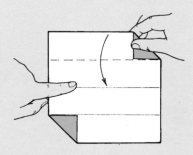

21 Once again, valley fold the top edge down to meet the middle fold-line.

24 Valley fold the top edge down to meet the lower horizontal fold-line. Press it flat and unfold it.

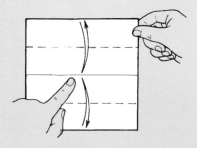

19 Valley fold the top and bottom edges to meet the middle fold-line. Press them flat and unfold them.

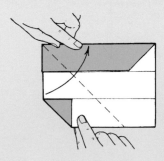

22 Valley fold the left-hand side up, so that it lies along the top edge.

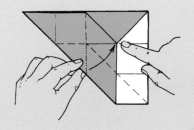

25 Put in the valley and mountain folds as shown, thereby making the left-hand corner stand upright.

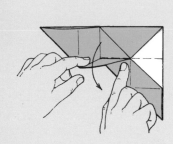

26 Valley fold the upright corner down towards you along the upper horizontal fold-line, thereby . . .

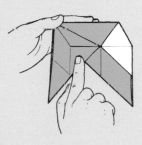

27 making the two sides stand upright and completing one unit of the base. Now make three more units in the same way.

Joining the Units Together

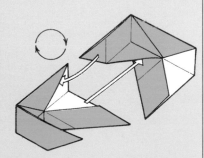

28 Insert one unit deep into the side pocket of another.

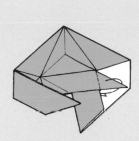

29 Lock both units together by tucking the point of the top unit underneath the point of the bottom unit.

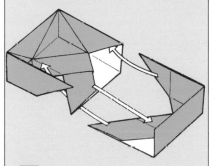

30 Repeat steps 28 and 29 with the remaining units.

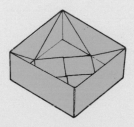

31 Here is the completed base.

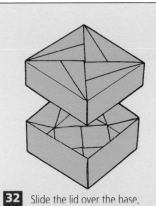

32 Slide the lid over the base, thereby . . .

33 completing the decorative box.

ACTION LIZARD

TOMOKO FUSE

As the various parts of the action lizard are made up of similar units, be very careful not to get the folding steps mixed up.

USE 12 SQUARES OF PAPER, IDENTICAL IN SIZE, WHITE SIDE UP.

Basic Unit

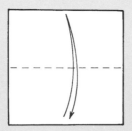

1 Valley fold one square in half from bottom to top. Press it flat and unfold it.

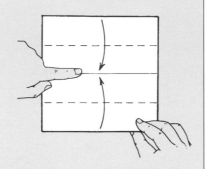

2 Valley fold the top and bottom edges to meet the middle fold-line, thereby . . .

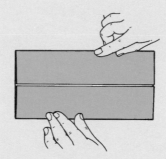

3 making a shape that in origami is called the cupboard fold.

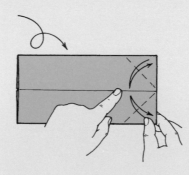

4 Turn the cupboard fold over. Valley fold the top and bottom right-hand corners over to meet the middle fold-line. Press them flat and unfold them.

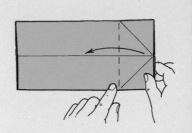

5 Valley fold the right-hand side over towards the left as shown, thereby making a flap.

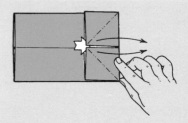

6 Open out the flap's two middle corners and . . .

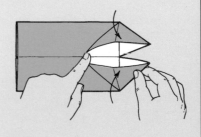

7 squash them down as shown, thereby . . .

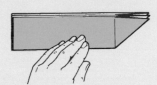

8 completing the basic unit. Now make eight more units in the same way.

11 completing one set of claws. Now make three more sets in the same way.

Body

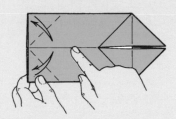

14 You will need three basic units. Valley fold one unit's top and bottom left-hand corners over to meet the middle fold-line. Press them flat and unfold them.

Claws

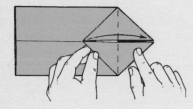

Head

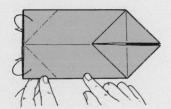

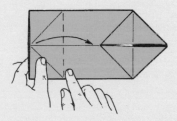

9 You will need four basic units. Valley fold one unit's triangular point over to the right as shown.

12 You will need one basic unit. Mountain fold the top and bottom left-hand corners behind to meet the middle fold-line, thereby . . .

15 Valley fold the left-hand side over towards the right as shown, thereby making a flap.

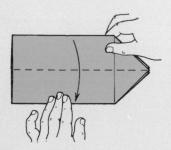

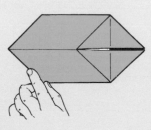

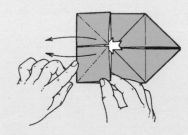

10 Valley fold the unit in half from top to bottom, thereby . . .

13 completing the head.

16 Repeat steps 6 and 7 with the flap, thereby . . .

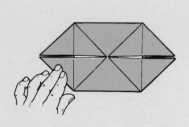

17 completing one body module. Now make two more modules in the same way.

Tail

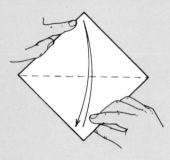

18 Turn one square around to look like a diamond. Valley fold it in half from bottom to top. Press it flat and unfold it.

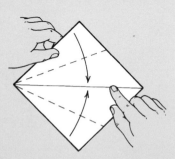

19 From the left-hand corner, valley fold the top and bottom sloping edges over to meet the middle fold-line, thereby making a shape that in origami is called the kite base.

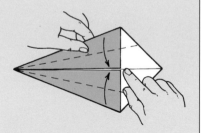

20 Once again, from the left-hand corner, valley fold the top and bottom sloping edges over to meet the middle fold-line, thereby . . .

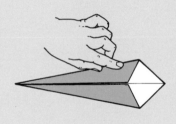

21 completing the tail.

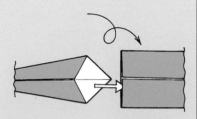

22 Turn the remaining basic unit over and tuck the tail deep inside it, . . .

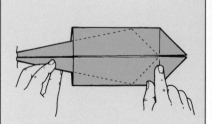

23 into the position shown by the dotted lines.

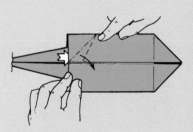

24 Pleat the top upper left-hand layer of paper, thereby . . .

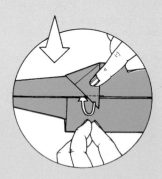

25 making a triangular point. With a mountain fold, tuck the point's tip inside the tail as far as you can.

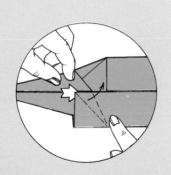

26 Repeat steps 24 and 25 with the top lower left-hand layer of paper, thereby . . .

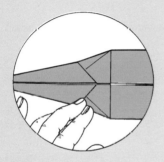

27 locking the tail in place.

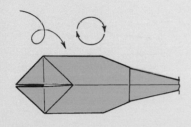

28 Finally, turn the tail over and around, into the position shown.

Front and Back Legs

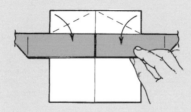

29 Front legs: Valley fold the opposite sides and top and bottom edges of one square together in turn to mark the vertical and horizontal fold-lines, then open up again.

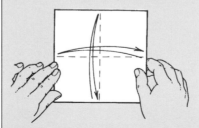

30 Place two sets of claws on top of the square, positioning them as shown, so that they lie above but adjacent to the horizontal fold-line. Valley fold the square's top corners over as shown.

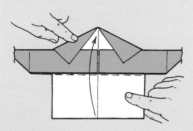

31 Valley fold the paper in half from bottom to top.

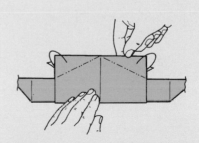

32 Mountain fold the top corners behind as shown, thereby locking the claws in place.

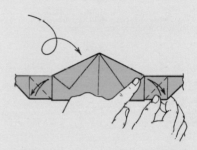

33 Turn the paper over. Valley fold each claw over to lie along its adjacent vertical edge. Press them flat and unfold them slightly.

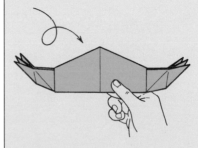

34 Turn the model over, thereby completing the front legs. To make the back legs, repeat steps 29 to 34 with the remaining square and claws.

How to Join the Lizard Together

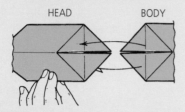

HEAD   BODY

35 Slot the head and one body module together as shown.

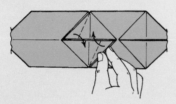

36 Valley fold the upper and lower triangular points over, so that their sloping edges lie along the adjacent fold-line, thereby making two flaps.

37 Insert the tip of each flap into the model as shown.

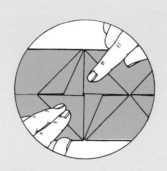

38 This should be the result.

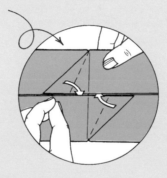

39 Turn the model over. Repeat steps 36 and 37.

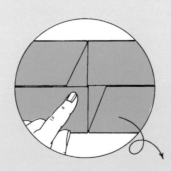

40 This should be the result: a movable joint. Turn the model over.

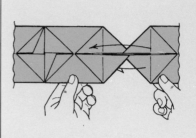

41 Repeat steps 35 to 40 with the remaining two body modules.

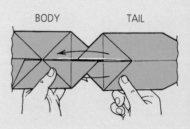

BODY   TAIL

42 Slot the tail and the body modules together as shown. Now repeat steps 36 to 40.

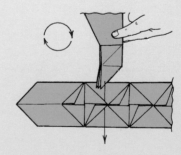

43 Turn the front legs around, into the position shown. Tuck them underneath the triangular points of the body module that is joined to the head.

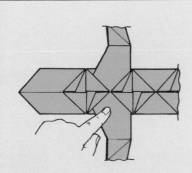

44 Make sure that the front legs are positioned centrally on top of the body module.

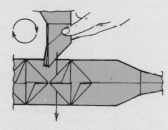

45 Turn the back legs around, into the position shown. Tuck them underneath the triangular points of the body module that is joined to the tail.

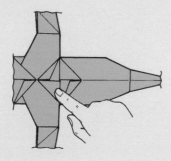

46 Repeat step 44 with the back legs.

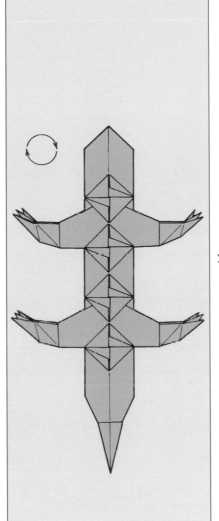

47 Turn the lizard around, into the position shown, to complete.

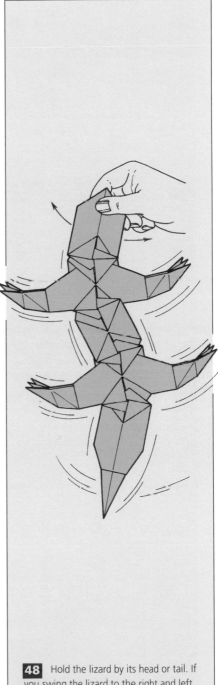

48 Hold the lizard by its head or tail. If you swing the lizard to the right and left, it will move and twist about.

PUZZLE ORIGAMI

As origami could be seen as a form of puzzle-solving, it is not
surprising that many origami enthusiasts also enjoy doing puzzles.
Especially for *The New Origami,* we have created a paper version of the
traditional tangram (see page 44). (This is a puzzle square that has been
divided into seven pieces. These pieces can be recombined to produce a
large variety of other shapes.) One paperfolder, Thoki Yenn, has
combined his knowledge of magic with that of origami to create an
almost impossible puzzle, which is even more amazing when you know
the solution (see page 56)!

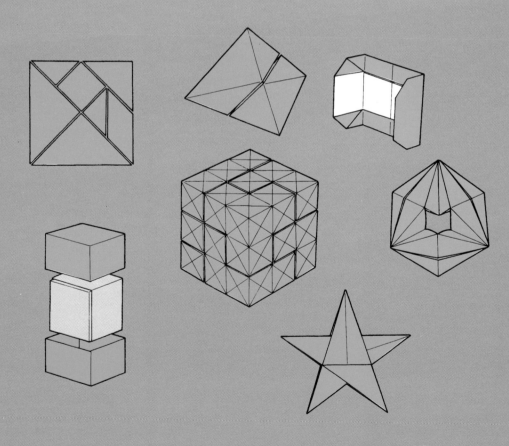

SOMA CUBE

(ORIGAMI VERSION)
INTRODUCED BY
STEVE BIDDLE

The soma cube was developed in 1936 by the Danish poet and puzzle creator Piet Hein. Many thousands of shapes and forms can be made from its seven pieces; in fact it can be likened to a three-dimensional version of the tangram (see page 44). This origami version of the soma cube is based on the traditional origami cube on page19. Once you have folded its seven pieces, see if you can fit them together in one large cube before you read the solution.

USE 122 SQUARES OF PAPER, IDENTICAL IN SIZE, WHITE SIDE UP. THE SOMA'S SEVEN PIECES ARE MADE BY TUCKING TOGETHER A COMBINATION OF DIFFERENT MODULES. THE FIVE MODULES ARE MADE AS FOLLOWS:

Module A

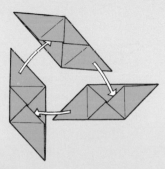

1 Begin by following steps 1 to 8 of the cube on page19, using every square of paper to make 122 units. To make module A, tuck three units together as shown.

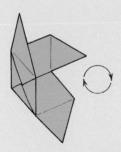

2 Turn the units around into the position shown, thereby completing module A.

Modules B and C

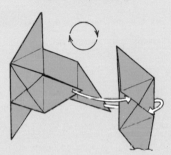

3 To make module B, begin by repeating steps 9 and 10 of the cube on page 20, with three units. Bend them around, into the position shown, to complete. To make module C, repeat this step with another three units. Tuck another unit into place as shown, thereby . . .

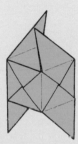

4 completing module C.

Module D

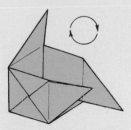

5 To make module D, begin by repeating steps 9 to 12 of the cube on page 20, using four units. Turn them around, into the position shown, to complete.

Module E

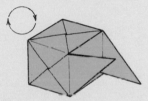

6 To make module E, begin by repeating steps 9 to 13 of the cube on page 20, using five units. Turn them around, into the position shown, to complete.

Joining the Modules Together

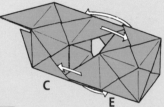

C

E

7 To make piece 1; you will need one module C, one module D, and two of module E. Tuck module C and one module E together as shown.

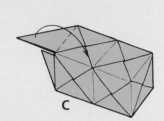

8 Valley fold the module C's top triangular point over towards the right.

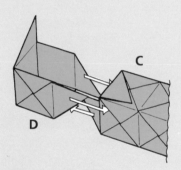

9 Tuck module D into place.

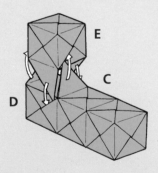

10 Stand module C's top triangular point upright and tuck the second module E into place as shown, thereby . . .

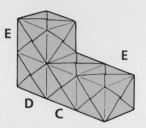

11 completing piece 1. The following six pieces are all constructed along similar lines.

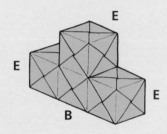

12 Piece 2: Tuck together one module B and three of module E, as shown.

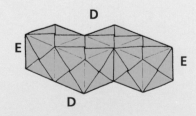

13 Piece 3: Tuck together two of module D and two of module E, as shown.

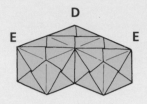

14 Piece 4: Tuck together one module D and two of module E, as shown.

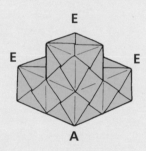

15 Piece 5: Tuck together one module A and three of module E, as shown.

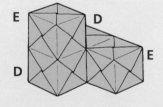

16 Piece 6: Tuck together two of module D and two of module E, as shown.

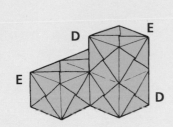

17 Piece 7: Tuck together two of module D and two of module E, as shown.

The Solution

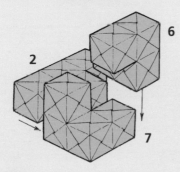

18 Place pieces 2, 6 and 7 together as shown.

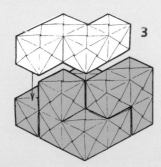

19 Place piece 3 into position.

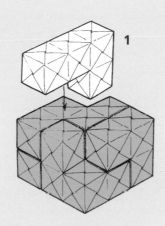

20 Carefully place piece 1 into position.

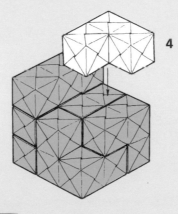

21 Carefully place piece 4 into position

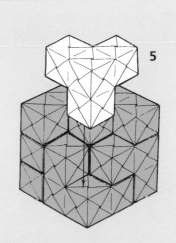

22 Finally, place piece 5 into position, thereby

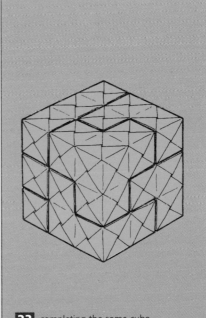

23 completing the soma cube.

When you have succeeded in making the cube, try devising other shapes of your own with the soma's seven pieces.

TANGRAM

(ORIGAMI VERSION)
STEVE BIDDLE

A tangram is a traditional puzzle that originated in China before the year 2000 BC. You can play with the puzzle, either by yourself or with friends, the aim being to rearrange its seven pieces in the shape of a square.

USE FIVE SQUARES OF PAPER, IDENTICAL IN SIZE, WHITE SIDE UP. YOU WILL ALSO NEED A PAIR OF SCISSORS.

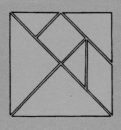

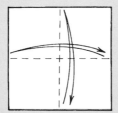

1 First make two large triangles. Valley fold the opposite sides and top and bottom edges of one square together in turn to mark the vertical and horizontal fold-lines, then open up again.

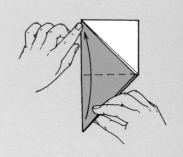

2 Valley fold the corners into the middle, thereby making a shape that in origami is called the blintz base.

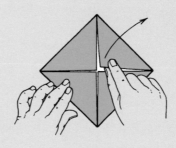

3 Unfold the top right-hand corner.

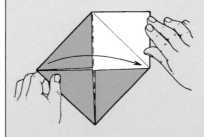

4 Valley fold the paper in half from left to right.

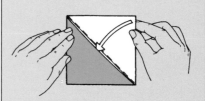

5 Valley fold the paper in half from bottom to top.

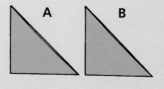

6 Tuck the top right-hand corner into the adjacent pocket, thereby . . .

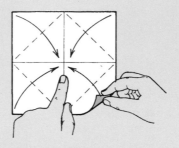

7 completing one large triangle. Repeat steps 1 to 6 with another square. Label the two triangles A and B.

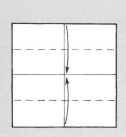

8 The next step is to make a parallelogram. Begin by repeating step 1 with one square. Valley fold the top and bottom edges to meet the middle fold-line.

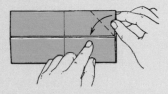

9 Valley fold the top right-hand corner over to meet the middle fold-line.

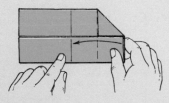

10 Valley fold the right-hand side into the middle.

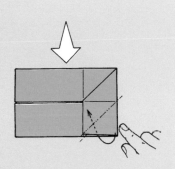

11 Inside reverse fold the bottom right-hand corner.

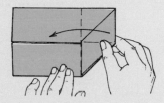

12 Valley fold the right-hand side over along the adjacent vertical fold-line.

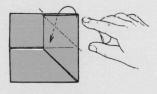

13 Inside reverse fold the top right-hand corner.

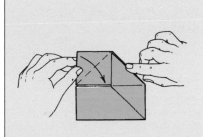

14 Valley fold the top left-hand corner over to meet the adjacent folded edge.

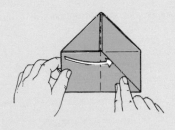

15 Insert the left-hand side underneath the right-hand layers of paper.

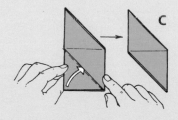

16 Insert the lower left-hand corner into the adjacent sloping pocket, thereby completing the parallelogram. Label the parallelogram C.

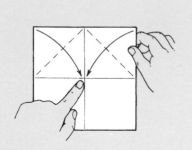

17 Next, make a square. Begin by repeating step 1 with one square. Valley fold the top corners into the middle, thereby making a shape that looks like the roof of a house.

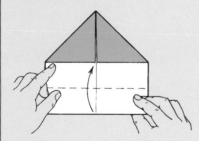

18 Valley fold the bottom edge to meet the roof's bottom edge.

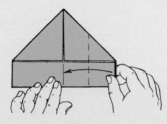

19 Valley fold the right-hand side over to meet the the middle fold-line.

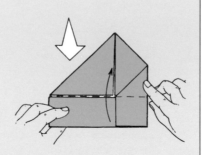

20 Valley fold the bottom edge up along the adjacent horizontal fold-line.

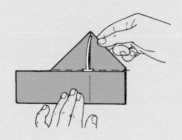

21 Insert the top point underneath the top layers of paper.

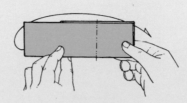

22 Along the existing vertical fold-line, mountain fold behind the left-hand section of paper.

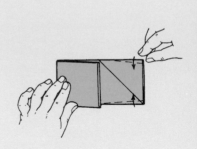

23 Valley fold the top and bottom right-hand edges over on a slant.

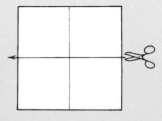

24 Valley fold the paper in half from right to left, inserting the right-hand side into the adjacent pocket to complete the square. Label the square D.

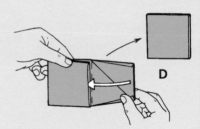

25 Finally, make one medium-sized triangle and two small triangles. Begin by repeating step 1 with the remaining square. Cut along the horizontal fold-line, thereby making two rectangles.

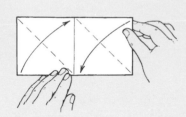

26 Place one rectangle sideways on. Valley fold the right-hand side down, so that it lies along the bottom edge. Valley fold the left-hand side up, so that it lies along the top edge.

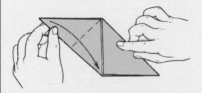

27 Valley fold the top left-hand point down to meet the bottom edge.

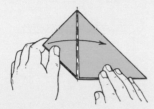

28 Valley fold the left-hand section of paper over along the adjacent vertical fold-line.

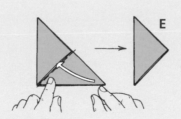

29 Insert the bottom right-hand point into the adjacent sloping pocket, thereby completing the triangle. Label this medium-sized triangle E.

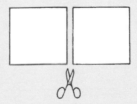

30 Cut the remaining rectangle in half along the vertical fold-line, thereby making two squares.

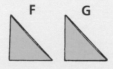

31 Repeat steps 1 to 7 with each square, thereby completing the small triangles. Label the two small triangles F and G.

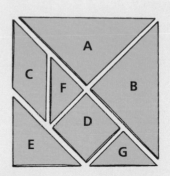

32 This is the tangram square. Shuffle the seven pieces, then try to rearrange them into a square without looking at this illustration.

33 Here are just two of the many different shapes you can make from the tangram square. Why not invent a few of your own?

TUMBLER

S T E V E   B I D D L E

This delightful and simple piece of action origami is based upon a model originally created by the late Seiryo Takekawa.

USE A RECTANGLE OF PAPER, A4 IN SIZE, WHITE SIDE UP.

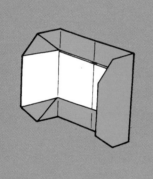

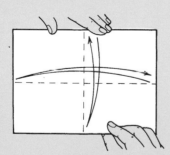

1 Place the rectangle sideways on. Valley fold the opposite sides and top and bottom edges together in turn to mark the vertical and horizontal fold-lines, then open up again.

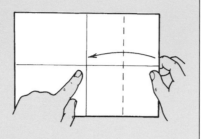

2 Valley fold the right-hand side into the middle.

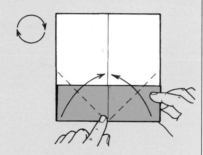

3 Turn the paper around into the position shown. Valley fold the bottom corners up to meet the middle fold-line, thereby making a shape that looks like an upside-down roof.

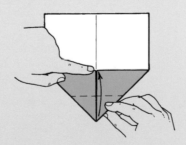

4 Valley fold the bottom point up to meet the roof's bottom edge.

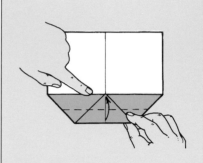

5 Valley fold the new bottom edge up to meet the roof's bottom edge.

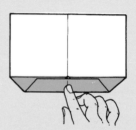

6 This should be the result.

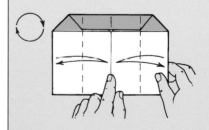

7 Turn the paper around, into the position shown. Valley fold the sides over to meet the middle fold-line. Press them flat and unfold them.

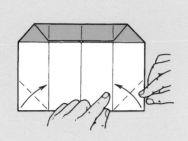

8 Valley fold the bottom corners in to meet their adjacent fold-lines as shown, thereby making two triangles.

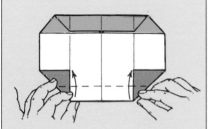

9 Valley fold the bottom edge up to lie along the top edges of the two triangles.

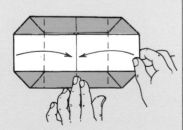

10 Once again, valley fold the sides over to meet the middle fold-line, thereby . . .

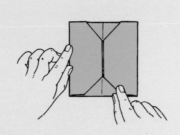

11 making two doors. Unfold the doors, so . . .

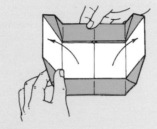

12 that they stand upright, thereby completing the tumbler.

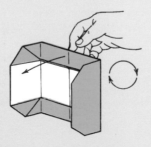

13 Stand the tumbler on a flat surface, with its doors facing away from you. Gently push its top edge with a finger, as shown, and this puzzling piece of origami will . . .

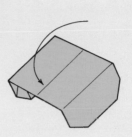

14 roll forwards, . . .

15 turning a somersault with a . . .

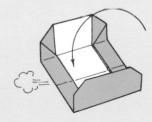

16 'rat-tat-tat'.

THE PYRAMID

DIDIER BOURSIN

This model is constructed from two identical pieces, which are put together to form a pyramid. This is not difficult - nor is it quite as easy as it sounds!

USE TWO RECTANGLES OF PAPER, A4 IN SIZE, WHITE SIDE UP.

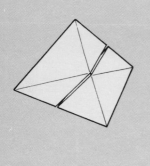

1   Place one rectangle sideways on. Divide it horizontally into three by folding, then open up again.

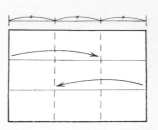

2   Valley fold the right-hand side over to a point one-third of the way from the left. Valley fold the left-hand side over so that it lies on top.

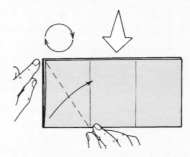

3   Turn the paper around, into the position shown. Valley fold the left-hand rectangle in half along one diagonal as shown.

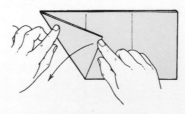

4   This should be the result. Press the paper flat and unfold it.

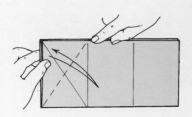

5   Valley fold the left-hand rectangle in half along its other diagonal. Press it flat and unfold it.

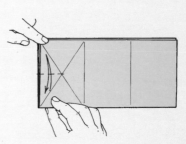

6   Valley fold the left-hand rectangle in half from bottom to top, being careful only to press on the paper from the rectangle's middle point to the side. Unfold it.

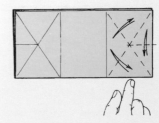

7   Repeat steps 3 to 6 with the right-hand rectangle.

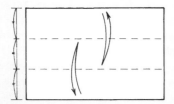

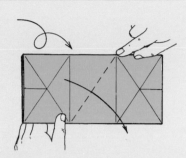

8 Turn the paper over. Valley fold the middle rectangle in half along a diagonal line from top right to bottom left.

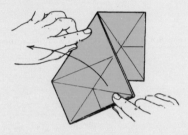

9 This should be the result. Press the paper flat and unfold it.

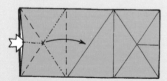

10 Stand the left-hand rectangle upright along the adjacent vertical fold-line. Using the existing fold-lines, open out the rectangle, taking . . .

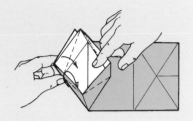

11 one layer of paper to one side and two to the other, as shown. Along the sloping fold-lines, push the two layered side inwards.

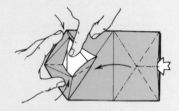

12 Bring the top and bottom points together, thereby making the paper become three-dimensional, at the same time producing a triangular flap. Repeat steps 10 to 12 with the right-hand rectangle.

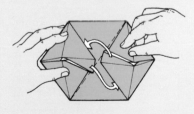

13 Position the triangular flaps so that the left-hand one points downwards and the right-hand one points upwards. Refold the middle rectangle's existing diagonal fold-line . . .

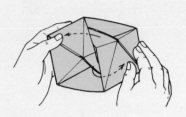

14 at the same time inserting the triangular flaps deep under the opposite sloping sides as shown.

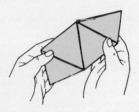

15 Firm up the folds, thereby completing one piece of the pyramid. Use the remaining rectangle of paper to make one more piece in the same way.

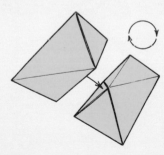

16 Turn the pieces around and place them together as shown to complete the pyramid.

ROTATING TETRAHEDRON

S T E V E   B I D D L E

This puzzle can be twisted so that various surfaces are revealed, thereby causing the pattern to change continuously.

USE A BOLDLY PATTERNED RECTANGLE OF PAPER, A4 IN SIZE, WHITE SIDE UP. YOU WILL ALSO NEED A PAIR OF SCISSORS.

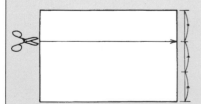

1 Place the rectangle sideways on. Cut off a third as shown and discard it.

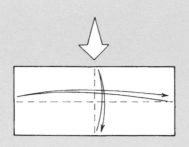

2 Valley fold the opposite sides and top and bottom edges together in turn to mark the vertical and horizontal fold-lines, then open up again.

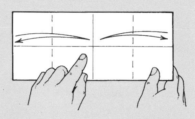

3 Valley fold the sides over to meet the middle fold-line. Press them flat and unfold them.

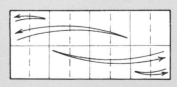

4 Divide the length into eight equal sections by valley folding.

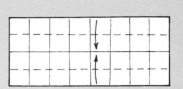

5 Valley fold the top and bottom edges to meet the middle fold-line.

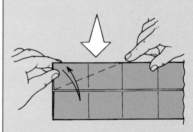

6 Working from the left-hand side and along the top edge, make a diagonal fold-line between the top of the second vertical fold-line and the left-hand end of the horizontal fold-line, as shown. Press the paper flat and unfold it.

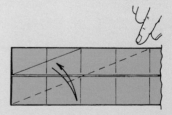

7 Repeat step 6, making the diagonal fold-line between the top of the middle vertical fold-line and the bottom left-hand corner as shown.

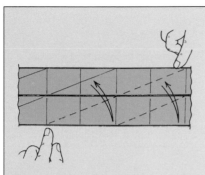

8 Continue repeating step 6 with the top edge, to the end of the paper, making five diagonal fold-lines, as shown in step 10.

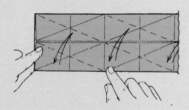

9 Working from the left-hand side, but this time along the bottom edge, repeat steps 6 to 8, ending with 10 diagonal fold-lines, as shown in step 10.

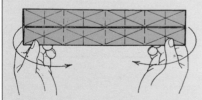

10 Bring the paper's right- and left-hand sides together by valley folding it as shown.

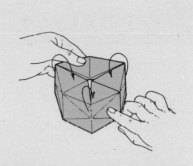

11 Insert one side inside the other, thereby making the model triangular and three-dimensional.

12 Push in the three triangular areas at the top of each side.

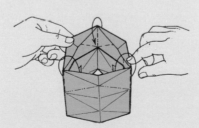

13 Press all three top points down and through the centre. The next row of triangles will assume a similar shape.

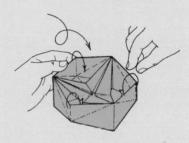

14 Once again, press all three top points down and through the centre.

15 Turn the model over. Repeat step 12, thereby . . .

16 completing the rotating tetrahedron. To make the model rotate, hold it on either side and twist the outer edges in towards the centre, so that the inner surfaces appear.

PENTAGRAM STAR

SHUZO FUJIMOTO

This is a very easy way to make a five-pointed star, with just a few folds. As always, fold carefully.

USE A RECTANGLE OF THIN PAPER, A4 IN SIZE, COLOURED ON BOTH SIDES.

1 Place the rectangle sideways on. Valley fold it in half from right to left.

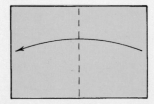

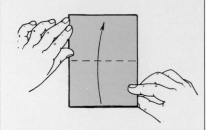

2 Valley fold the paper in half from bottom to top.

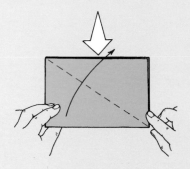

3 Valley fold the paper along a line from top left to bottom right.

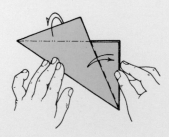

4 Mountain fold the top sloping edge and valley fold the right-hand side as shown. Press them flat and unfold them.

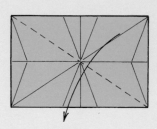

5 Unfold the paper completely. Valley fold the the paper along a line from top left to bottom right.

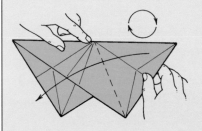

6 Turn the paper around, into the position shown. Valley fold the top right-hand point over on a line between the middle of the top edge and the bottom right-hand point.

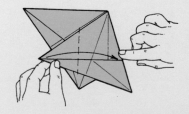

7 Valley fold the left-hand point over to meet the right-hand sloping side as shown.

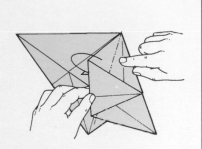

8 Along the existing fold-line, mountain fold the paper as shown. In doing so, let the point swing across to the left.

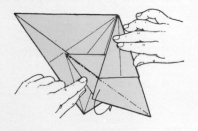

9 Along the existing fold-line, mountain fold the paper as shown.

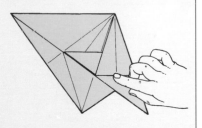

10 This should be the result.

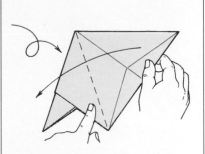

11 Turn the model over. Valley fold the top right-hand point over on a line between the top left-hand point and the bottom right-hand point.

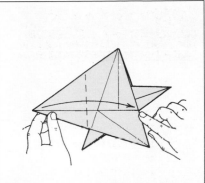

12 Repeat steps 7 to 9, thereby . . .

13 completing the pentagram star.

INSIDE-OUTSIDE BOX

THOKI YENN

A red box is displayed. Its lid is removed and a blue box is seen to be fitting snugly inside. The blue box is removed. The lid is replaced on the red box.
Now . . . are you ready for this? The lid from the blue box is removed, the red box is placed snugly inside the blue box and the lid is replaced on top of the blue box! A really quite impossible puzzle.

USE FOUR RECTANGLES OF PAPER, A4 IN SIZE, WHITE SIDE UP. (TRY USING TWO RED PIECES OF PAPER FOR ONE BOX AND TWO BLUE PIECES FOR THE OTHER.)

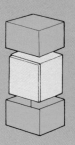

Base

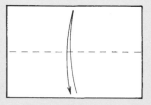

1 Place one rectangle sideways on. Valley fold it in half from bottom to top. Press the paper flat and unfold it.

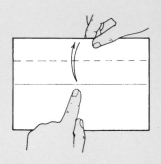

2 Valley fold the top edge down to meet the middle fold-line. Press it flat and unfold it.

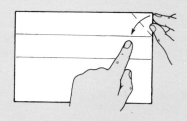

3 Valley fold the top right-hand corner over to meet the adjacent fold-line.

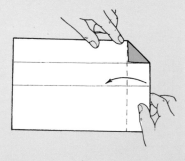

4 Valley fold the right-hand side over as shown.

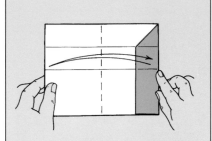

5 Valley fold the paper in half from right to left. Press it flat and unfold it.

0.5 cm

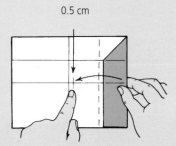

6 Valley fold the right-hand side over to a point that is 0.5 cm (¼ inch) to the right of the fold-line made in step 5.

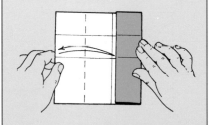

7 Valley fold the left-hand side over to meet the vertical folded side, as shown. Press it flat. Unfold the paper completely.

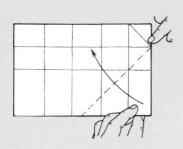

8 Valley fold the bottom right-hand corner up to meet the top horizontal fold-line as shown.

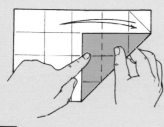

9 Refold the right-hand side along the second vertical fold-line. Press it flat and unfold it.

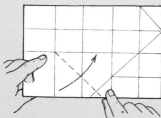

10 Unfold the paper completely. Working from the left, valley fold the first vertical fold-line over to lie along the middle horizontal fold-line, only pressing down on the part of the fold shown by the line of dashes.

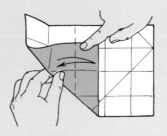

11 Once again, working from the left, refold the left-hand side along the second vertical fold-line. Press it flat. Unfold the paper completely.

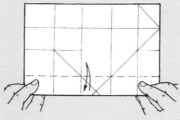

12 Valley fold the bottom edge up along the adjacent horizontal fold-line, thereby creasing the missing middle piece of the fold. Press it flat and unfold it.

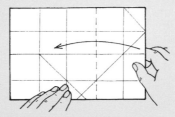

13 Refold the right-hand side along the second vertical fold-line.

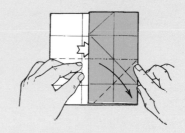

14 On the top right-hand layer of paper, make the valley and mountain folds as shown, thereby opening it out and making the underneath layer of paper rise up along the middle horizontal fold-line to form the back and right-hand side of the base.

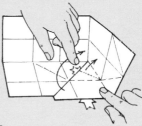

15 Form the valley and mountain folds on the bottom flap of paper as shown, thereby creating a small triangle that will come to rest against the base's side.

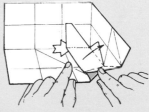

16 Open out the bottom flap of paper and push its top layer against the base's back and right-hand side, thereby covering up the small triangle.

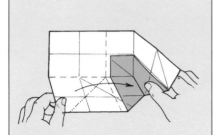

17 On the left-hand side of the paper, carefully make the valley and mountain folds as shown, thereby forming the left-hand side of the base. Repeat step 15, . . .

18 thereby creating a small triangular flap in front. Insert the flap into the model as shown.

19 Valley fold the top edge down along the adjacent horizontal fold-line.

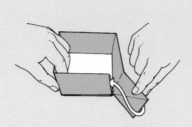

20 Insert the right-hand flap of paper into the adjacent pocket, thereby . . .

21 completing the base.

Lid

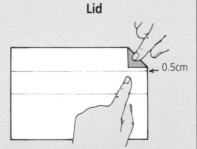

← 0.5cm

22 Repeat steps 1 to 21 with an identical coloured rectangle of paper, but being careful in step 3 to fold the top right-hand corner over to a point that is 0.5 cm (¼ inch) above the adjacent fold-line. The remaining folding procedure is exactly the same as for the base.

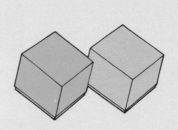

23 Slide the lid over the base, thereby completing one box. Make another box with the remaining two rectangles of paper.

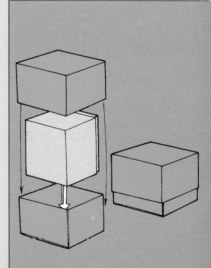

24 Nesting of boxes: Inner box fully closed. The outer box cannot close completely because its length is larger than its depth. It is possible to put either box inside the other because the boxes have identical dimensions.

STORYTELLING ORIGAMI

Opportunities to combine origami with storytelling present themselves whenever people are gathered together. The showing of origami is a rewarding experience; onlookers of all ages are filled with rapture and wonder as models take shape or transform from one to another in the storyteller's hands.

When developing an origami story, it is a good idea to write the model's folding sequence down in the form of a list, then to develop your script, no matter how improbable, around these representations.

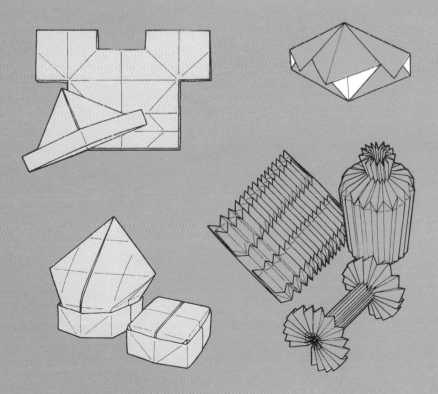

PAPER PUPPET

RACHEL KATZ

Even with the best illustrations, some people will have trouble with particular steps. To solve this problem, the creator of this delightful action model has written a story that gives a descriptive name to each move or shape. Here is Rachel's story, written as she would tell it.

USE A SQUARE OF PAPER, WHITE SIDE UP.

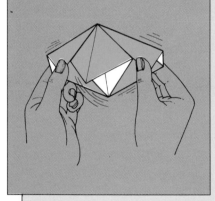

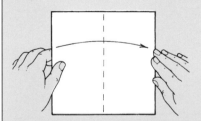

1   One day as I was putting my book away . . .
(Valley fold the square in half from left to right. Press it flat . . .

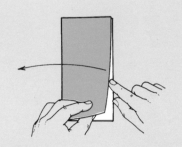

2   and unfold it.)

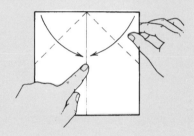

3   I went into my house and started to play.
(Valley fold the top corners down to meet the middle fold-line.)

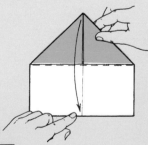

4   That's when I found this . . .
(Valley fold the paper in half from top to bottom.)

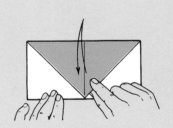

5   envelope and letter. 'Fold me some more,' it said. 'You can do better.'

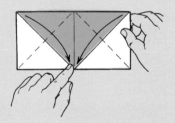

6   I folded the top down and . . .
(Valley fold the top corners down to meet the middle fold-line.)

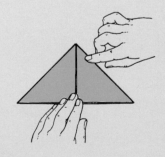

7   made a good crease.
(Press the paper flat.)

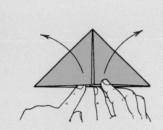

8 'Open up! It's the . . .
(Unfold the model back to . . .

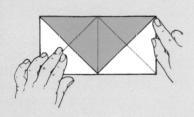

9 origami police.'
the envelope and letter.)

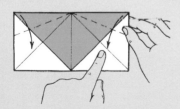

10 'Now fold it just half-way.'
(Valley fold the top corners down to meet the . . .

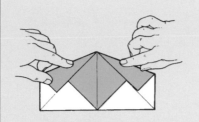

11 'No more should you dare.'
sloping fold-lines.)

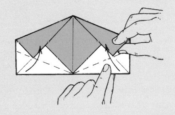

12 'And fold the bottom . . .
(Valley fold the bottom corners up to meet the sloping folded edges, while at the same time . . .

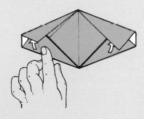

13 can you see up to where?'
inserting them underneath the top corners as shown.)

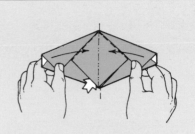

14 'Then hold it and push it, and here's what you say . . .
(Hold the side points, bring them towards each other, and make the middle section of paper rise up along the existing fold-lines.)

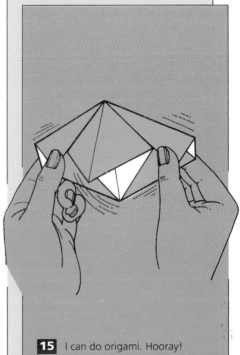

15 I can do origami. Hooray! Hooray!'
(Open and close the side points to make the puppet 'talk'.)

THE CAPTAIN'S HAT STORY

TRADITIONAL

To accompany the folding of this traditional paper hat, the late Lillian Oppenheimer told the story of how a child's hat became first a boat and then the captain's shirt. Read on to find out what happens!

USE A COMPLETE DOUBLE-PAGE SHEET FROM A BROADSHEET (LARGE-SIZED) NEWSPAPER.

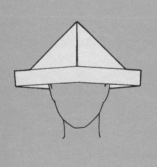

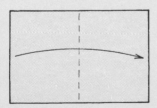

1 Valley fold the sheet of newspaper in half along its middle fold.

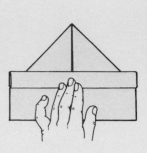

2 Turn the newspaper around, so that the folded edge is along the top. Valley fold the newspaper in half from side to side. Press it flat and unfold it.

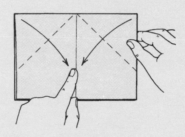

3 Valley fold the top corners down to meet the middle fold-line.

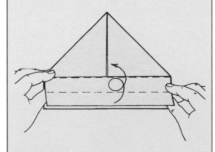

4 Valley fold the front flap at the bottom up to meet the horizontal edge and then over along the edge.

5 This should be the result.

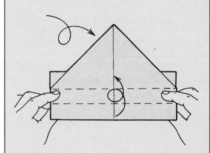

6 Turn the paper over. Repeat step 4.

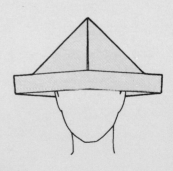

7 Press the paper flat. Open out the paper a little, thereby making the captain's hat.

8 Hold the back and front edges of the hat in either hand and pull them apart, thereby . . .

9 collapsing the hat . . .

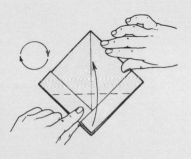

10 into this new shape. Position the model as shown and valley fold the bottom point of the front flap up.

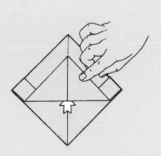

11 Repeat step 7, thereby . . .

12 making the fireman's hat.

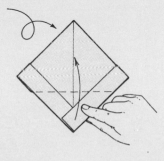

13 Press the paper flat again and turn it over. Valley fold the bottom point of the front flap up, so that it matches the one behind.

14 Repeat steps 8 and 9, thereby . . .

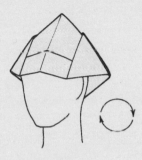

15 making the explorer's hat.

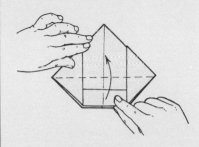

16 Press the paper flat again. Valley fold the front flap at the bottom up on a line between the two side points, as shown.

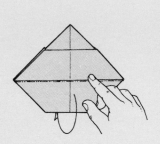

17 Mountain fold the back flap at the bottom behind on a line between the two side points.

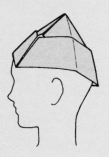

18 Repeat step 7, thereby making the pirate's hat.

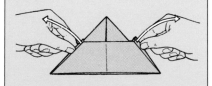

19 Press the paper flat again. Pinch the two side points and pull them apart, thereby . . .

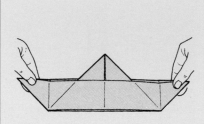

20 making the traditional newspaper boat.

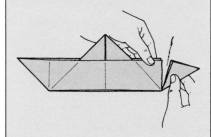

21 Now you begin to tell the story. There is a storm at sea. In the storm, the boat loses its stern and bow. (You tear the side points off as shown.)

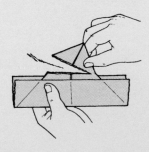

22 It also loses the bridge. (You tear the top point off.)

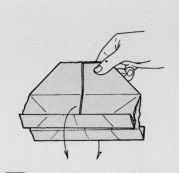

23 Now there is . . . (Start to unfold what is left.)

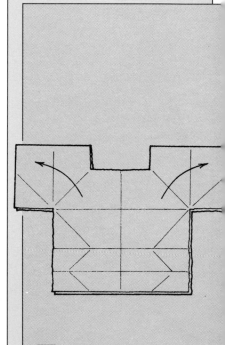

24 nothing left but the captain's shirt!

PRINTER'S HAT

(TRADITIONAL)

In this folding routine, a hat folded from a sheet of newspaper is changed into various other types of hat.

USE A COMPLETE DOUBLE-PAGE SHEET FROM A BROADSHEET (LARGE-SIZED) NEWSPAPER.

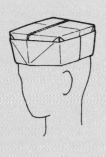

1 Begin by following steps 1 to 5 of the captain's hat on page 62, using the sheet of newspaper.

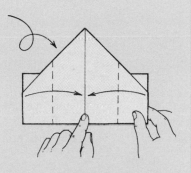

2 Turn the paper over. Valley fold the sides over to meet the middle fold-line.

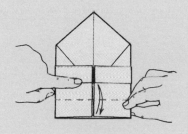

3 Valley fold the flap up to meet the adjacent horizontal edge. Press it flat and unfold it.

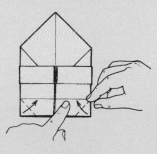

4 Valley fold the bottom corners over to meet the fold-line made in step 3.

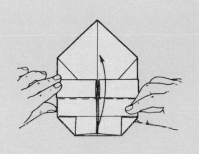

5 Valley fold the flap up along the adjacent horizontal edge.

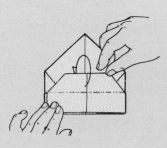

6 Mountain fold the flap along the fold-line made in step 3, inserting it behind the underneath layers of paper.

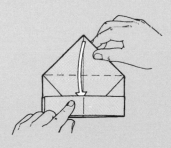

7 Valley fold the top point down, inserting it underneath all the layers at the bottom.

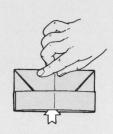

8 Open out the paper a little, thereby . . .

9 making the party hat.

10 Turn the hat over. Hold the front and back edges of the hat in either hand and pull them apart, thereby . . .

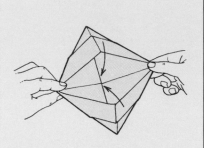

11 collapsing the paper . . .

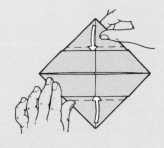

12 into this new shape. Valley fold the top and bottom points into the middle and insert them underneath the horizontal bands of paper.

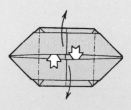

13 Put your fingers inside the paper. Gently pull your hands apart. The paper will . . .

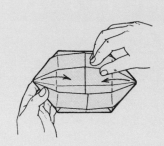

14 start to open out into a box.

15 Pinch the corners and sides of the box together to make it firm and strong

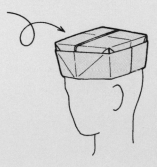

16 Turn the box over, thereby making the printer's hat.

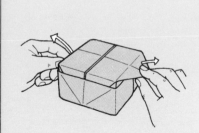

17 Pull out the two side points from the band of paper. Arrange them so that they lie flat, sticking out beyond the band, thereby . . .

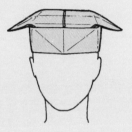

18 making the jester's cap.

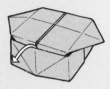

19 Pull out the front point from the band of paper. Arrange it so that it lies flat, sticking out beyond the band, thereby . . .

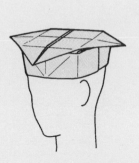

20 making the mortar-board.

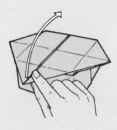

21 Pull the mortar-board's front point straight up, thereby . . .

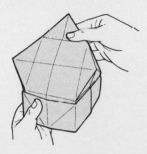

22 making the bishop's mitre.

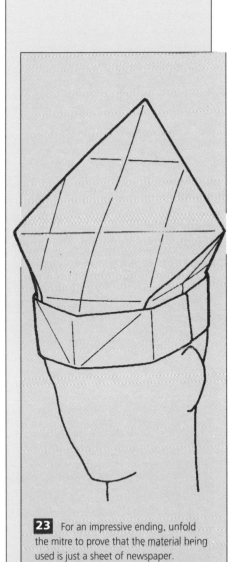

23 For an impressive ending, unfold the mitre to prove that the material being used is just a sheet of newspaper.

TROUBLEWIT

(TRADITIONAL) INTRODUCED BY STEVE BIDDLE

One of the earliest types of entertainment to be recorded in China was the art of folding and pleating a rectangle of paper in different ways, so that, when manipulated by the performer, it could be assembled in an assortment of different shapes. About 300 years ago, a French priest, Père Mathieu, took this paperfolding art from China to France. In France, it had different names, *Papier Multiforme* being the most popular. It was in England, during the last century, that this art became known as 'Troublewit'.

USE A RECTANGULAR PIECE OF STRONG CARTRIDGE OR WATERCOLOUR PAPER, MEASURING 48 X 64 CM (19 X 25 INCHES).

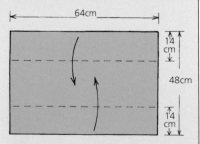

1   Place the rectangle sideways on. Valley fold the top and bottom edges over as shown, thereby making two panels of paper.

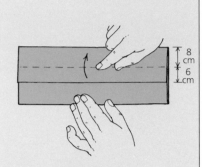

2   Valley fold the upper panel over along a horizontal line that is 8 cm (3 inches) down from the top edge.

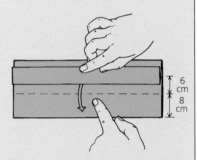

3   Valley fold the lower panel over along a horizontal line that is 8 cm (3 inches) up from the bottom edge.

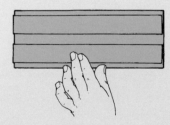

4   This should be the result - three panels either side with a strip in the middle.

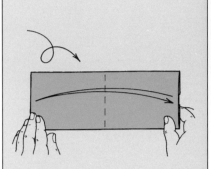

5   Turn the paper over. Valley fold the paper in half from side to side. Press it flat and unfold it.

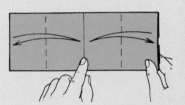

6   Valley fold the sides over to meet the middle fold-line. Press them flat and unfold them.

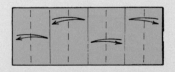

7   Divide the length into eight equal sections by valley folding. Press the folds flat and unfold them.

8 Divide the length into 16 equal sections by valley folding. Press the folds flat and unfold them.

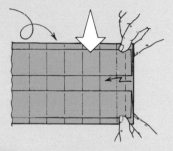

9 Turn the paper over. From one end, pleat the length into 32 equal sections by valley and mountain folding. Note that the mountain folds take place along existing fold-lines.

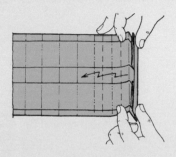

10 Take great care with the pleating, and make sure that your folding is neat, sharp, with pleats registering perfectly one over the other.

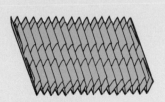

11 This should be the result, one long pleated strip of paper, rather like an accordion.

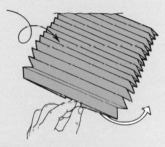

12 Turn the paper over. Now comes one of the trickiest bits of all – making the troublewit's angled corners. Take the right-hand folded edge that lies across the middle of the pleated strip and carefully ease it out, until it stands at an angle of 90° to the main part.

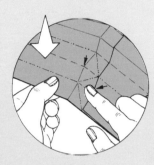

13 Carefully reverse fold the angled corners into shape, and . . .

14 press the folds firmly together as shown.

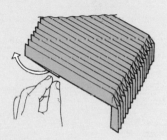

15 Now take the left-hand folded edge and carefully ease this out in the same way. As before, reverse fold the angle corners into shape.

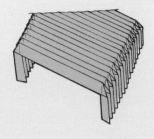

16 This should be the result.

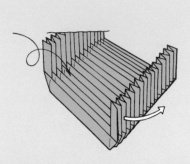

17 Turn the structure over. Now take the right-hand raw edge and carefully ease it out, until it stands at an angle of 90° to the main part.

18 Repeat step 13 at the point where the pleats cross.

19 Repeat step 14.

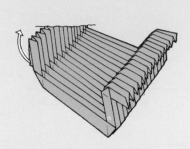

20 Now take the left-hand raw edge and carefully ease this out in the same way. As before, reverse fold the angled corners into shape.

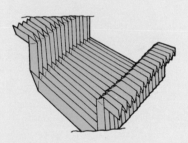

21 This should be the result: a completed troublewit.

22 To sharpen the folds, lay the troublewit on its side and place a heavy book or two on top to compress it.

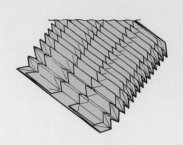

23 When step 22 has been done satisfactorily, fold the troublewit back into position, as shown.

24 Here is the first and simplest shape, the fan.

25 The ribbon is made by holding the troublewit in the middle as shown.

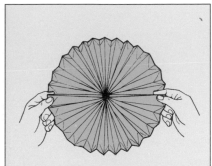

26 With the troublewit closed as in step 23, the rosette is made by bringing the top and bottom of each side panel together.

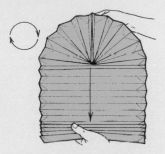

27 Let one side of the rosette go, and you will have what looks like a church window. From now on, you can devise many hundreds of shapes. Each basic fold of the paper will provide you with a new shape.

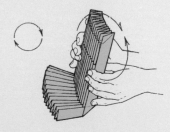

28 First Basic Fold: This shows the troublewit with one panel eased out and pressed together. Bring the front and back vertical panels round and together, thereby . . .

29 making the candle stick.

30 Second Basic Fold: This shows the troublewit with two panels eased out and pressed together. Bring the front and back horizontal panels together in the direction shown by the arrows, thereby . . .

31 making the dumb-bell.

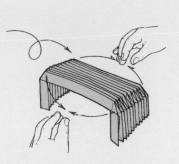

32 Turn the Second Basic Fold over and bring the vertical panels together as shown, thereby . . .

33 making the birthday cake.

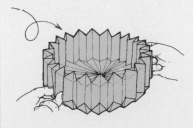

34 Turn the birthday cake over to make the cake tin.

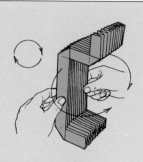

35 Third Basic Fold: This shows the troublewit with three panels eased out and pressed together. Turn the troublewit around into the position shown, then bring the front and back vertical panels together, thereby . . .

36 making the bottle.

37 Go back to the Third Basic Fold and bring the vertical panels together in the opposite direction to make the glass.

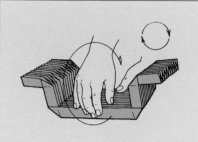

38 Fourth Basic Fold: This shows the troublewit with four panels eased out and pressed together. Turn the troublewit around into the position shown and take the front horizontal panel around to the back, thereby. . .

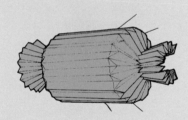

39 making the bonbon.

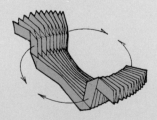

40 With the troublewit in this position, bring the vertical panels together and hold in place, thereby . . .

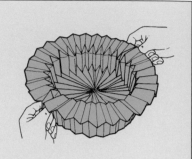

41 making the sweet dish.

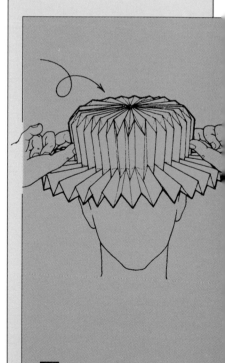

42 To complete, turn the sweet dish over to make the beefeater's hat.

PRACTICAL ORIGAMI

Many letter folds, envelopes and other useful items have been developed in origami, perhaps because it is an intriguing technical challenge to try to create pockets into which loose flaps can be inserted. Many different origami wallets and containers have also been designed to hold business cards, sheets of paper, a gift or pencils.

In 1988, John Cunliffe, a British paperfolder with an interest in practical origami, founded the Envelope and Letterfold Association with the aim of circulating information amongst those with similar interests.

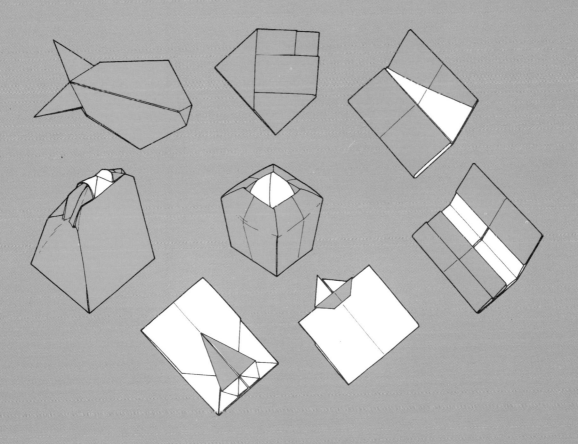

BAMBOO LETTERFOLD

(TRADITIONAL) INTRODUCED BY TAKENAO HANDA

This traditional, elegant model is an ideal way of folding up a letter.

USE AN A-SIZED RECTANGLE OF PAPER, WHITE OR WRITTEN SIDE UP.

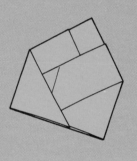

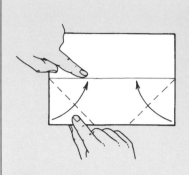

2 Valley fold the two bottom corners up to meet the middle fold-line.

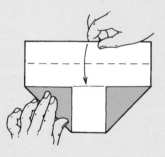

3 Valley fold the top edge down to meet the middle fold-line.

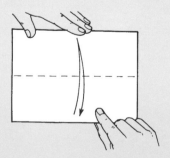

1 Place the rectangle sideways on. Valley fold the rectangle in half from bottom to top. Press it flat and unfold it.

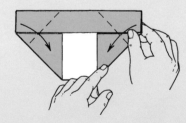

4 Valley fold the top corners down to meet the vertical edges as shown.

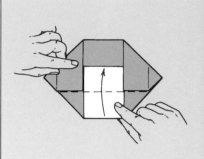

5 Valley fold the bottom edge up to meet the horizontal edge.

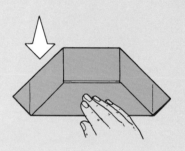

6 This should be the result.

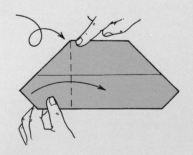

7 Turn the paper over. Valley fold the left-hand corner over on a vertical line as shown.

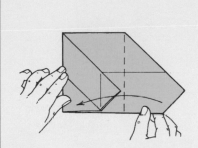

8 Valley fold the right-hand corner over on a vertical line as shown, and . . .

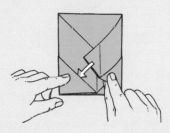

9 insert it underneath the opposite sloping edge.

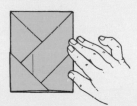

10 This should be the result.

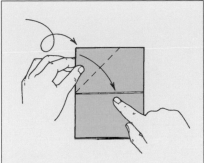

11 Turn the paper over. Valley fold the top left-hand corner down to meet the horizontal edges.

12 Valley fold the top right-hand corner down to meet the horizontal edges, and . . .

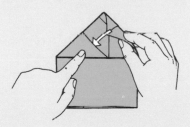

13 insert it underneath the opposite sloping edge.

14 This should be the result.

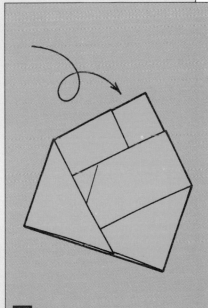

15 Turn the paper over, thereby completing the bamboo letterfold.

FISH LETTERFOLD

MICHEL GRAND

Here is a very novel way of folding up a letter.

USE AN A-SIZED RECTANGLE OF PAPER, WHITE OR WRITTEN SIDE UP.

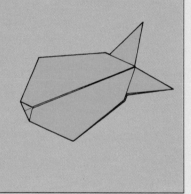

1 Place the rectangle sideways on. Valley fold it along a line from top left to bottom right.

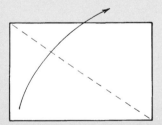

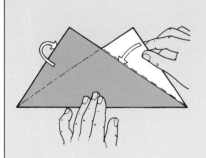

2 Mountain and valley fold the edges down into the model along the line of the adjacent sloping edges, as shown, thereby making a triangle.

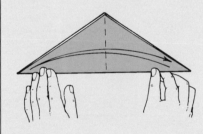

3 Valley fold the triangle in half from side to side. Press it flat and unfold it.

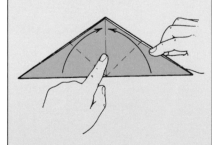

4 Valley fold the right- and left-hand halves of the bottom edge up to meet the middle fold-line.

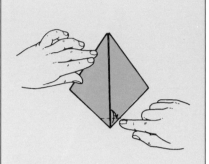

5 Valley fold up a little of the bottom point. Press it flat and unfold it.

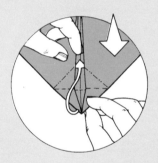

6 Using the fold-line made in step 5 as a guide, insert the bottom point into the model as shown.

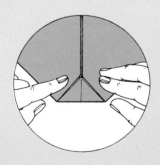

7 This should be the result.

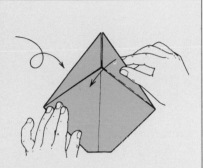

8 Turn the model over. Valley fold the top right-hand point over along the adjacent sloping edge.

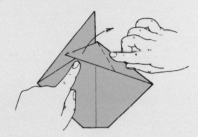

9 Shape the right-hand fin with a valley fold.

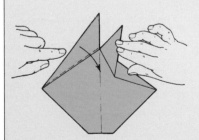

10 Without turning the model over, repeat steps 8 and 9 with the top left-hand point.

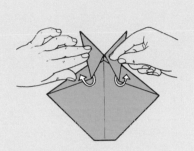

11 Insert the fins down inside the model, by going between the front and back layers of paper.

12 Inside reverse fold the two side points at the angle as shown.

13 Separate the front layer of paper from the back one.

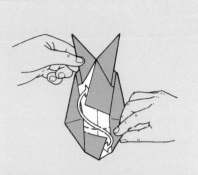

14 Insert one inside flap into the other as shown, while at the same time . . .

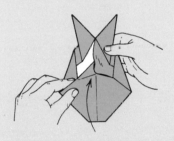

15 folding the separated layers back together. Press them flat, thereby . . .

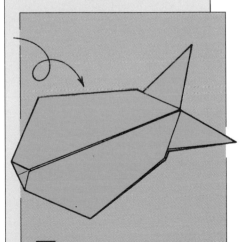

16 completing the fish letterfold.

FANCY WALLET

MEGUMI BIDDLE

This model was originally created to be folded from a long gift towel, but it is just as effectively made from paper. The wallet makes use of pleating and provides endless possibilities for variations.

USE A RECTANGLE OF PAPER, 3 X 1 IN PROPORTION, COLOURED SIDE UP.

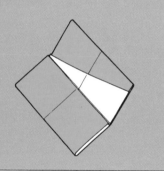

1 Place the rectangle sideways on. Valley fold the opposite sides and top and bottom edges together in turn to mark the vertical and horizontal fold-lines, then open up again.

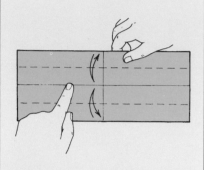

2 Valley fold the top and bottom edges over to meet the middle fold-line. Press them flat and unfold them.

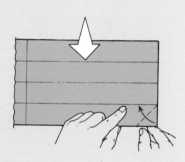

3 Valley fold the bottom right-hand corner over to meet the adjacent fold-line, thereby making a small triangle.

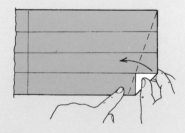

4 Valley fold the right-hand side over on a line between the top right-hand corner and the small triangle's tip.

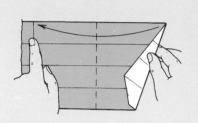

5 Valley fold the top right-hand corner over to meet the middle fold-line.

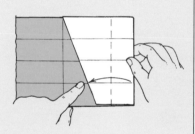

6 Valley fold the right-hand side over to the place at which the sloping edge and . . .

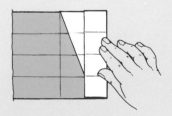

7 the lower horizontal fold-line intersect.

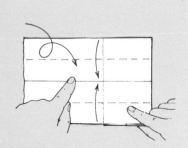

8 Turn the paper over. Valley fold the top and bottom edges over to meet the middle fold-line.

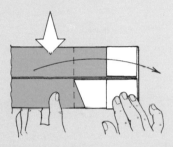

9 Valley fold the left-hand side of the paper over to the right, along what was originally the middle fold-line.

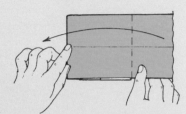

10 Using the underneath right-hand side as a guide to the position of the fold-line, valley fold the right-hand side of the paper over to the left.

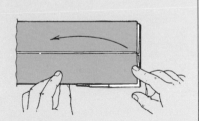

11 Press the paper flat. Unfold the last two steps.

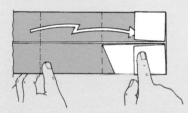

12 Along the existing fold-lines, pleat the paper as shown, at the same time inserting the pleat underneath the top right-hand layers of paper.

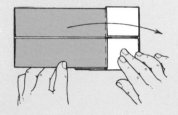

13 Using the vertical folded edges as a guide to the position of the fold-line, valley fold the top layer of paper over to the right.

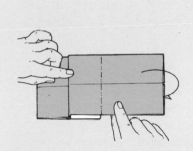

14 Using the underneath right-hand side as a guide to the position of the fold-line, mountain fold the top layer of paper behind.

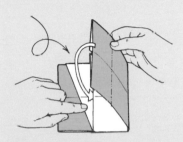

15 Turn the model over. Insert the top layer of paper into the model as shown.

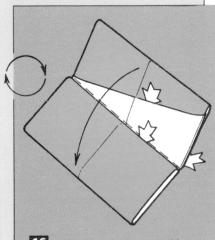

16 Valley fold the model in half from top to bottom, thereby completing the fancy wallet. The arrows indicate the various pockets that the wallet contains.

FLOWER VASE

SABURO KASE

This charming model makes an ideal container for all sorts of small items, such as paper clips, pens and pencils. Try changing the angle of the fold-lines in step 7 each time you make this model to see how many different flower vases you can create.

USE A SQUARE OF PAPER, WHITE SIDE UP.

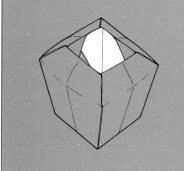

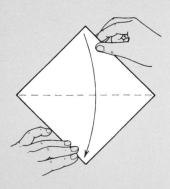

1 Turn the square around to look like a diamond. Valley fold it in half from top to bottom, thereby making a triangle.

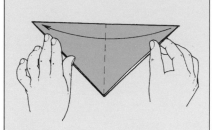

2 Valley fold the triangle in half from right to left.

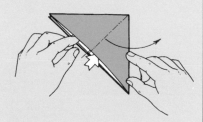

3 Lift the top half up along the middle fold-line. Open out the paper and . . .

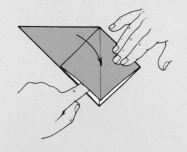

4 squash it down neatly into a diamond.

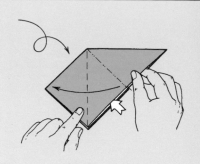

5 Turn the paper over, then repeat steps 3 . . .

6 and 4, thereby making a shape that in origami is called the preliminary fold.

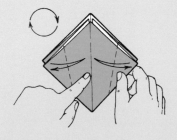

7 Turn the preliminary fold around, so that the open layers are pointing away from you. Valley fold the top right and left side points over to meet the middle fold-line as shown. Press them flat and unfold them.

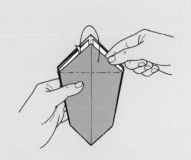

8 Using the fold-lines made in step 7 as a guide, inside reverse fold the side points . . .

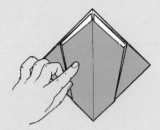

9 into the model. Press them flat.

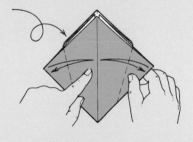

10 Turn the model over. Without turning it around, repeat steps 7 to 9.

11 Mountain fold the top point into the model . . .

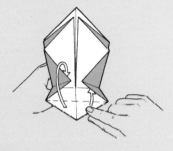

12 covering the small inner flap on the left-hand side and going underneath the flap on the right-hand side.

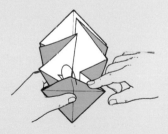

13 This shows steps 11 and 12 taking place.

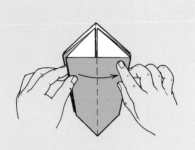

14 Valley fold the left-hand flap over to the right, as though turning the page of a book.

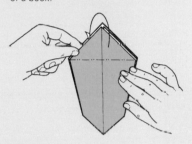

15 Repeat steps 11 to 13.

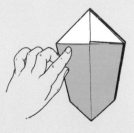

16 This should be the result.

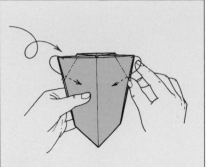

17 Turn the model over. Repeat steps 11 to 15.

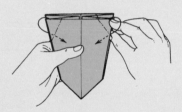

18 Inside reverse fold the top corners as shown.

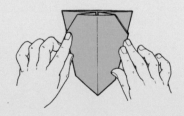

19 This should be the result.

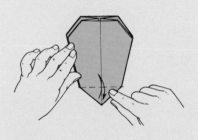

20 Turn the model over, then repeat step 18.

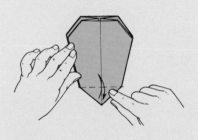

21 Valley fold the bottom point over as shown. Press it flat and unfold it.

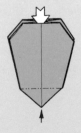

22 Using the fold-line made in step 21 as a guide, flatten the bottom point of the model by . . .

23 placing a finger inside the model at the top and carefully pushing out the four sides of the vase.

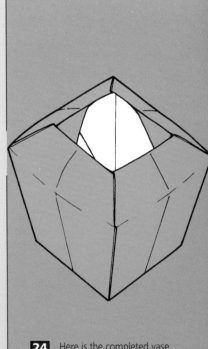

24 Here is the completed vase.

WALLET

MARTIN WALL

You will find this model ideal for carrying small items, such as postage stamps and business cards.

USE A RECTANGLE OF PAPER, A3 IN SIZE, COLOURED SIDE UP.

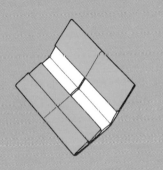

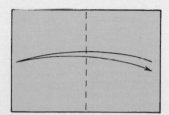

1 Place the rectangle sideways on. Valley fold it in half from side to side. Press the paper flat and unfold it.

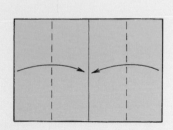

2 Valley fold the sides over to meet the middle fold-line.

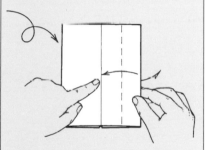

3 Turn the paper over. Valley fold the right-hand side over to meet the middle fold-line, while at the same time . . .

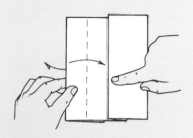

4 letting the paper from underneath flick up. Without turning the paper over, repeat steps 3 and 4 with the left-hand side.

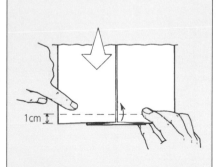

1cm

5 Valley fold the bottom edge up along a horizontal line that is 1 cm (½ inch) away from the bottom edge.

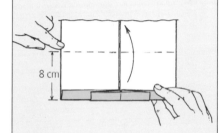

8 cm

6 Repeat step 5, but valley fold the edge up along a horizontal line that is 8 cm (3 inches) away from the bottom edge.

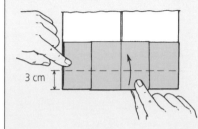

3 cm

7 Again repeat step 5, but valley fold the edge up along a horizontal line that is 3 cm (1¼ inches) away from the bottom edge.

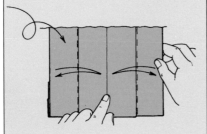

8   This should be the result.

9   Turn the paper over. Valley fold the sides over to meet the middle fold-line. Press them flat and unfold them.

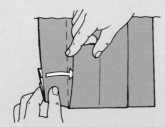

10   Using the fold-line made in step 9 as a guide, insert the left-hand side underneath the . . .

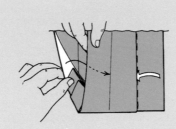

11   adjacent vertical folded side as shown. Repeat steps 10 and 11 with the right-hand side.

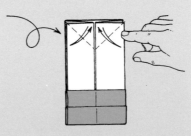

12   This should be the result.

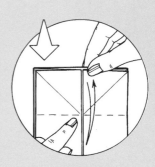

13   Turn the paper over. Valley fold the middle corners over, so that they lie along their adjacent sides. Press them flat and unfold them.

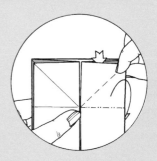

14   Valley fold the top edge down along a line where the fold-lines made in step 13 and the vertical middle edges intersect. Press it flat and unfold it.

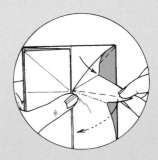

15   Using the fold-lines made in steps 13 and 14 as a guide, inside reverse fold the 'upper' right-hand corner down . . .

16   in between the adjoining layers of paper.

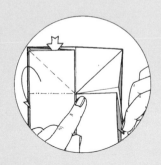

17 This should be the result. Press the paper flat. Repeat steps 15 to 17 with the 'upper' left-hand corner.

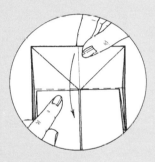

18 Valley fold the top edge down along the adjacent horizontal folded edge, at the same time . . .

19 inserting the two side points behind their adjacent sloping edges as shown.

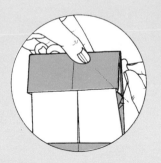

20 Mountain fold the 'hidden' right-hand point (that is to be found in between the front and back layers of paper) . . .

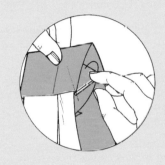

21 down as far . . .

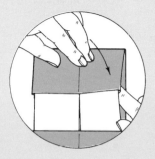

22 as it will go. Repeat steps 20 to 22 with the 'hidden' left-hand point.

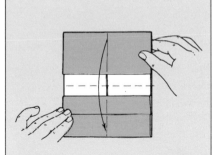

23 Valley fold the model in half from top to bottom, thereby completing the wallet.

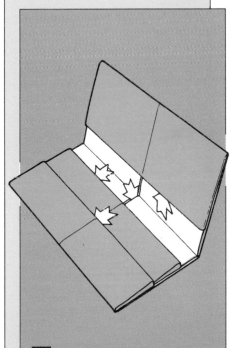

24 Here is the wallet in its opened position. The arrows indicate the various pockets that the wallet contains.

TREE ENVELOPE

JOHN CUNLIFFE

Many paperfolders like to fold models on a single theme, and John Cunliffe is no exception. He has created many items that could be considered 'practical' origami.

USE A SQUARE OF PAPER, COLOURED SIDE UP.

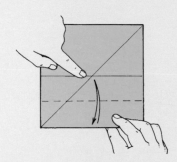

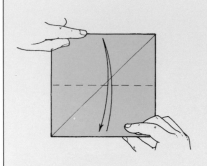

2 Valley fold the square in half from bottom to top. Press it flat and unfold it.

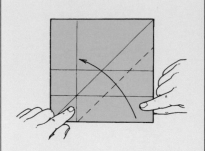

5 Valley fold the bottom right-hand corner up to meet the fold-line made in step 4.

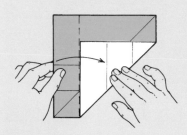

3 Valley fold the bottom edge up to meet the middle fold-line. Press it flat and unfold it.

6 Along the existing vertical fold-line, refold the left-hand side.

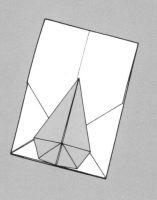

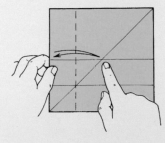

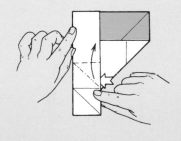

1 Valley fold the square in half from bottom right to top left. Press it flat and unfold it.

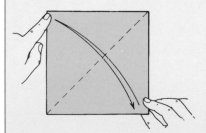

4 Valley fold the left-hand side to where the fold-lines intersect. Press it flat and unfold it.

7 Lift the lower left-hand section of paper up, open it out . . .

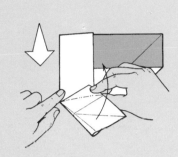

8 and squash it down as shown, thereby making a flap of paper.

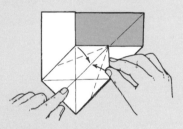

9 From the flap's top point, valley fold the top and bottom sloping edges to meet the middle fold-line.

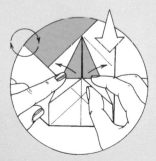

10 Turn the flap around, into the position shown. Unfold the sloping edges

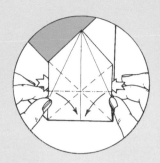

11 Place a finger against the flap's sides, and . . .

12 using the existing fold-lines as a guide, bring the sides together . . .

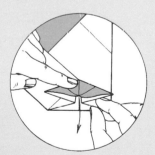

13 and down towards you. Press the paper down neatly, thereby making it diamond-shaped.

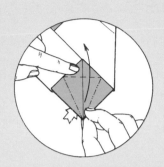

14 Lift up the diamond's bottom point, and . . .

15 using the fold-lines made in step 9, push in its edges so that they meet in the middle. (This origami technique is known as a petal fold.)

16 Press the paper flat, thereby making a tree-like shape.

17 Mountain fold the top left-hand corner down behind itself.

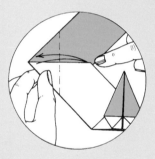

18 Valley fold the left-hand side point to where the newly made folded edge and sloping edge intersect. Press it flat and unfold it.

19 Open out the folded edge and squash down the paper as shown, thereby making a triangular flap.

20 Valley fold the left-hand side over to meet the middle fold-line, at the same time inserting the triangular flap . . .

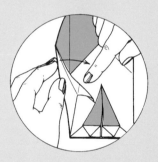

21 behind the adjacent sloping edge, as shown.

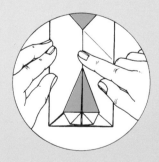

22 This should be the result. Press the paper flat.

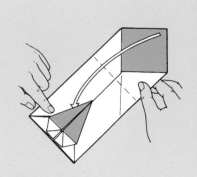

23 Valley fold the top point down and insert it behind the 'tree', thereby . . .

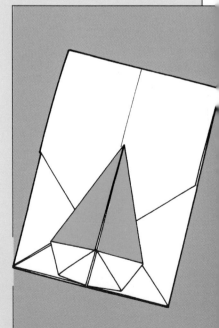

24 completing the tree envelope.

GIFT BAG

VINCENT FLODERER

This gift bag is very easy to make and can look very decorative. It can be made in many different sizes. Once you have learned the basic technique, many variations are possible.

USE A LARGE A-SIZED RECTANGLE OF PAPER, (SEE PAGE 16), WHITE SIDE UP.

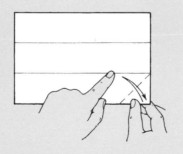

2 Valley fold the bottom right-hand corner over to meet the adjacent fold-line. Press it flat and unfold it.

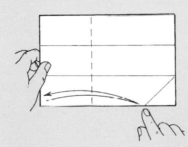

3 Valley fold the left-hand side over to where the bottom edge and the fold-line made in step 2 intersect. Press it flat and unfold it.

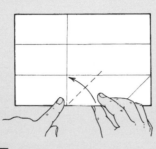

4 Valley fold the bottom edge over to meet the vertical fold-line, being careful to . . .

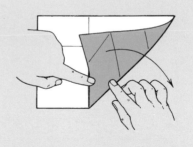

5 press the paper only as shown by the line of dashes in step 4. Unfold it.

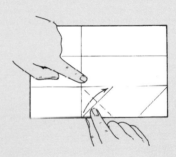

6 Valley fold the lower third of the vertical fold-line over to meet the adjacent horizontal fold-line, as shown. Press it flat and unfold it.

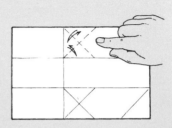

7 Repeat steps 4 and 5 with the top edge, and step 6 with the upper third of the vertical fold-line.

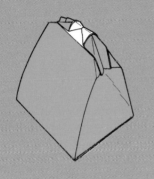

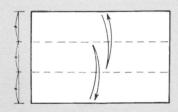

1 Place the rectangle sideways on. Divide it horizontally into three by folding, then open it up again.

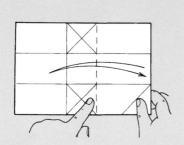

8 Valley fold the right-hand side over towards the left as shown. Press it flat and unfold it.

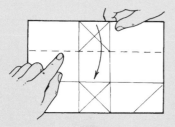

9 Valley fold the top edge over along the adjacent horizontal fold-line.

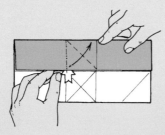

10 Using the existing fold-lines, open out the paper as shown, thereby making it stand upright.

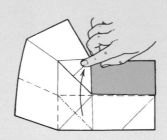

11 Repeat steps 9 and 10 with the bottom edge.

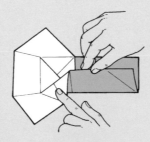

12 This should be the result.

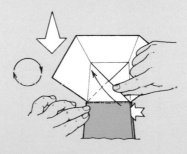

13 Turn the paper around, into the position shown. Again, using the existing fold-lines, open out the top layer of paper.

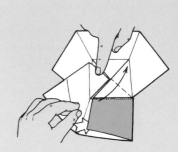

14 Once again, using the existing fold-lines, open out the remaining layer of paper, thereby . . .

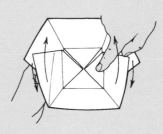

15 making a box-like shape.

16 Place your gift inside. Push the box's sides inwards, so . . .

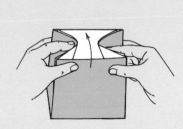

17 that they lie flat, at the same time bringing the front and back edges together as shown.

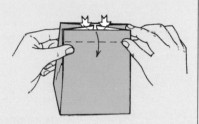

18 Treating the top three layers of paper as if they were one, valley fold them down, so that . . .

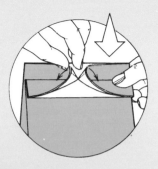

19 the inside layers rise up. Flatten the folded edge of each layer to form squash folds.

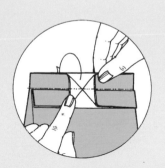

20 Treating the remaining top three layers of paper as if they were one, mountain fold them behind.

21 Mountain fold the top right- and left-hand corners on a slant down between the front and back layers of paper.

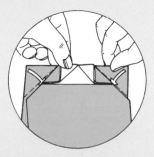

22 Valley fold the remaining top corners on a slant down between the front and back layers of paper, thereby . . .

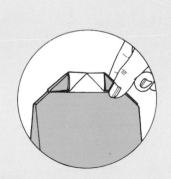

23 closing up the top of the gift bag.

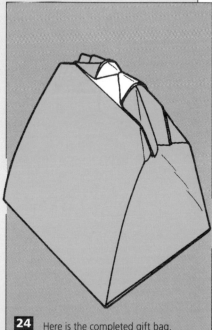

24 Here is the completed gift bag.

SAILING BOAT NOTEFOLD

STEVE BIDDLE

This model is based on the traditional origami sailing boat. It would make the ideal invitation note for a party.

USE A SQUARE OF PAPER, COLOURED SIDE UP.

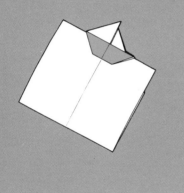

1 Turn the square around to look like a diamond. Valley fold the opposite corners together in turn to mark the diagonal fold-lines, then open up again.

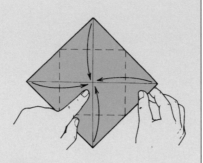

2 Valley fold the corners into the middle, thereby making a blintz base.

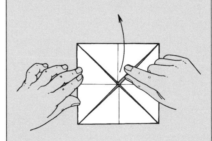

3 Unfold one middle corner as shown.

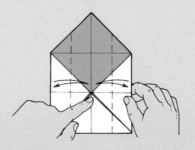

4 Valley fold the sides over to meet the middle fold-line. Press them flat and unfold them.

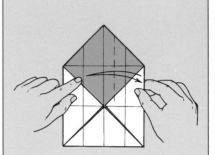

5 Valley fold the right-hand side over to meet the left-hand vertical fold-line made in step 4. Press the paper only as shown by the line of dashes, then unfold it.

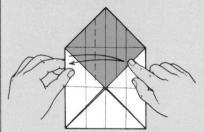

6 Valley fold the left-hand side over to meet the right-hand vertical fold-line made in step 4. Press the paper only as shown by the line of dashes, then unfold it.

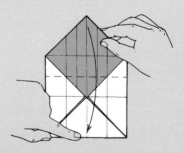

7 Valley fold the paper in half from top to bottom, thereby making a flap.

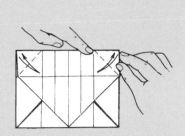

8 Valley fold the top corners over to meet their adjacent vertical fold-lines. Press them flat and unfold them.

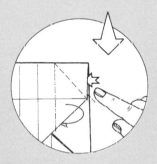

9 Along the existing fold-lines, mountain fold the flap's right-hand edge behind itself, at the same time . . .

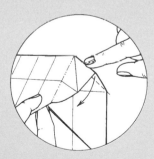

10 inside reverse folding the top right-hand corner down into the model, as shown.

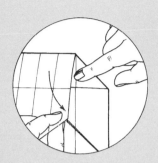

11 This should be the result. Repeat steps 9 and 10 with the top left-hand corner.

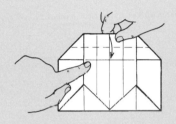

12 Valley fold the top edge over to meet the adjacent horizontal fold-line.

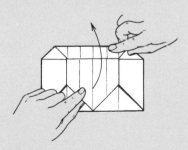

13 Lift up the flap, thereby making the inside layers rise up.

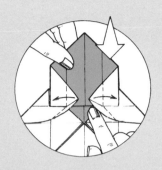

14 Flatten each layer to either side as shown.

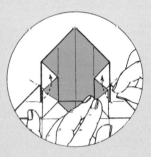

15 Valley fold the flap's concealed corners over.

16 This shows step 15 taking place.

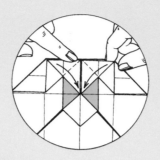

17 Turn the model over. Valley fold the flap's sides over to meet the middle fold-line, at the same time . . .

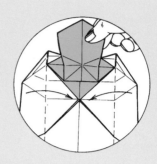

20 Valley fold the two side points over to meet the middle fold-line.

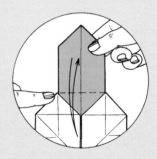

23 Valley fold the sides over to meet the middle fold-line.

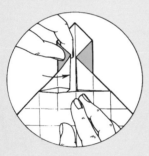

18 opening out the concealed corners.

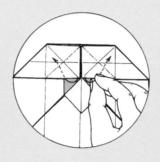

21 Inside reverse fold the side points up into the model.

24 Valley fold the flap down on a line between the two side points, as shown. Press it flat and unfold it.

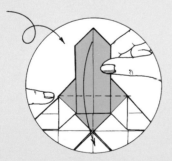

19 Turn the model over. Valley fold the flap down on a line between the two side points, as shown.

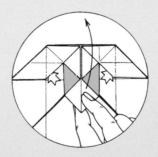

22 Lift up the flap, thereby making the sides rise up along the fold-lines made in step 4.

25 Valley fold the flap's right-hand side over to meet the fold-line made in step 24. Press it flat and unfold it. Repeat with the flap's left-hand side.

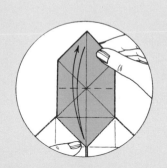

26 Valley fold the flap in half. Press it flat and unfold it.

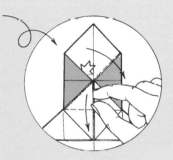

27 Turn the model over. Using the existing fold-lines, open out and squash down the flap's left-hand side as shown.

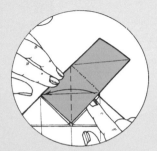

28 Using the existing vertical fold-line, valley fold the flap over to the left, thereby . . .

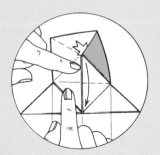

29 making it stand upright. Once again, using the existing fold-lines, open out the flap's right-hand side. Press the paper down neatly, thereby making a triangular flap that points to the left.

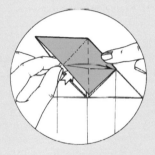

30 Open out the triangular flap and squash it down neatly into a diamond.

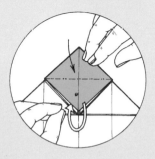

31 Mountain fold the diamond's bottom point up behind itself to the top, thereby making an upside-down sailing boat shape.

32 Shape the boat's hull with a mountain fold.

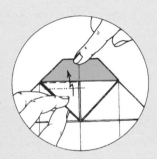

33 Step fold the boat's left-hand sail, thereby making a pleat.

34 Insert the pleat inside the boat.

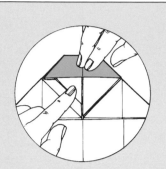

35 This should be the result.

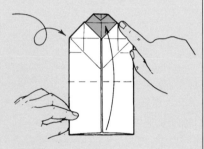

36 Turn the model over. Valley fold the bottom edge up to meet the fold-line made in step 24, at the same time . . .

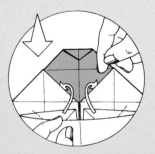

37 inserting the bottom two middle points behind their adjacent sloping edges, as shown.

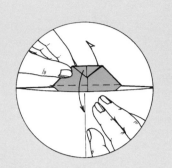

38 Swing the sailing boat around . . .

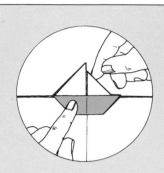

39 to the front. Press the paper flat, thereby . . .

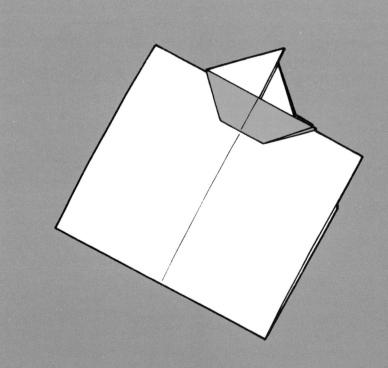

40 completing the sailing boat notefold.

KASANE ORIGAMI

Kasane origami is the name given to 'layered paperfolding'. It is a technique in which several (four or more) sheets of differently coloured paper are overlayed so that 'ribbons' of different colours run along either one edge or two adjacent edges. These overlayed sheets are then treated as a single item and folded together in the final stages of making the model. This technique is perfect for folding stylized items, such as Hina Ningyo (traditional costumed dolls) and Tato (folded paper purses).

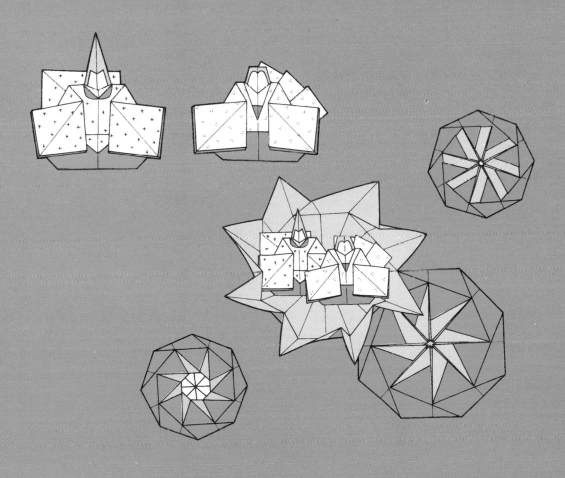

HINA NINGYO

(TRADITIONAL)
INTRODUCED BY
MEGUMI BIDDLE

The dimensions given in the instructions for making this model are only approximate as traditionally they were measured by eye and only personal experience can tell you how far to cut and fold.

FOR EACH DOLL, USE FOUR 15 CM (6-INCH) SQUARES OF PAPER OF THE FOLLOWING COLOURS: PATTERNED, COLOURED, WHITE AND BLACK. YOU WILL ALSO NEED A PAIR OF SCISSORS, A PENCIL AND A RULER.

Emperor

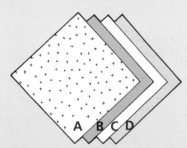

1 As a help during assembly, label the squares with a pencil as follows: patterned A, coloured B, white C and black D. Arrange the four squares as shown, with the coloured/patterned sides on top.

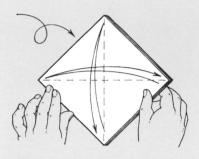

2 Treating the squares as if they were one, turn them over. Valley fold the opposite corners together in turn to mark the diagonal fold-lines, and open them up.

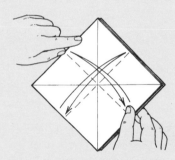

3 Again, treating the squares as if they were one, valley fold the opposite sides and edges together in turn to mark the vertical and horizontal fold-lines, and open them up.

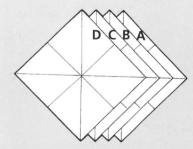

4 This should be the result. Separate the squares from each other.

D

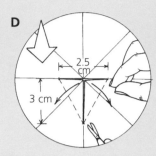

5 To make the various collars, cut each square as shown. Square D: In the square's middle and along its diagonal fold-lines, make a T-shaped cut, with a width of 2.5 cm (1 inch) and a length of 3 cm (1¼ inches). Valley fold the middle corners over, on . . .

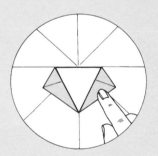

6 a line between the top and bottom of the 'T'.

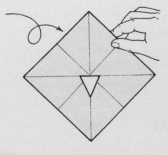

7 Turn the paper over.

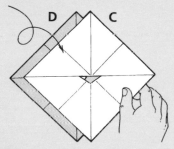

8 Square C: Repeat steps 5 and 6, but make a T-shaped cut with a width of 2.5 cm (1 inch) and a length of 1 cm (½ inch).

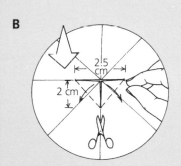

9 Turn square C over and place it on top of square D.

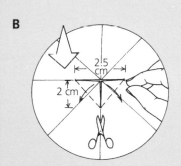

10 Square B: Repeat steps 5 and 6, but make a T-shaped cut with a width of 2.5 cm (1 inch) and a length of 2 cm (¾ inch).

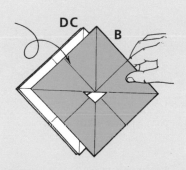

11 Turn square B over and place it on top of squares C and D.

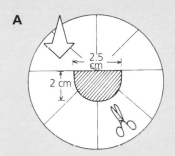

12 Square A: In the square's middle and along its diagonal fold-lines, cut out a U-like shape, with a width of 2.5 cm (1 inch) and a length of 2 cm (¾ inch). Discard the shaded part.

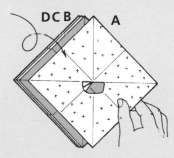

13 Turn square A over and place it on top of squares B, C and D.

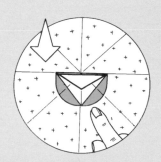

14 Make sure that the squares are arranged as in step 1. You should now be able to see the various collars.

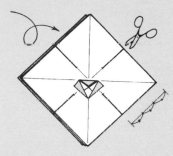

15 Treating the squares as if they were one, turn them over. Again, treating the squares as if they were one, from the middle of each edge and side, cut two-thirds of the way to the middle. Separate the squares from each other.

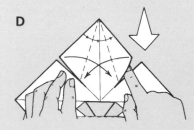

16 Square D: From the top corner, valley fold the right-hand sloping edge over one-third of the way, as shown. Repeat with the left-hand sloping edge, so . . .

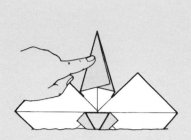

17 that it lies on top and makes a point as shown.

18 Turn the paper over. In the point's topmost layer, make a V-shaped cut, as shown.

C

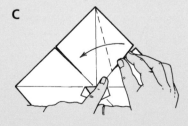

19 Square C: From the top corner, valley fold the right-hand sloping edge over as far as possible.

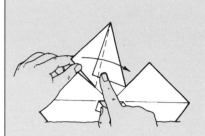

20 Repeat step 19 with the left-hand sloping edge.

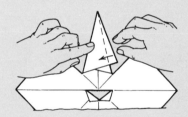

21 Valley fold the protruding right-hand flap over and towards the left on a line with the underneath sloping edge, so . . .

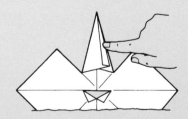

22 that it lies on top and makes a point as shown.

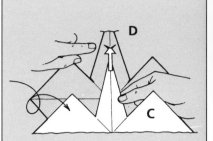

23 Turn square C over and insert its point into the V-shaped cut of square D's point. Push the point up inside as far as it will go, thereby making the Emperor's head.

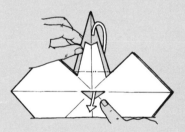

24 Mountain fold and insert the head into the triangular hole. You may have to enlarge the hole slightly first.

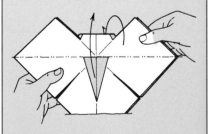

25 Treating both squares as if they were one, make the horizontal mountain fold as shown, at the same time . . .

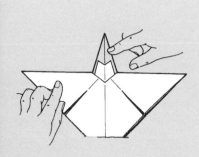

26 letting the head flip around to the top.

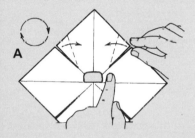

27 Square A: Turn the paper around, into the position shown. Valley fold the side corners of the top section of paper in on a slant.

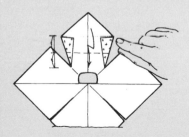

28 Step fold the top section of paper as shown.

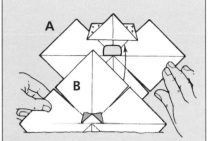

29 Square B: Turn the paper around, into the position shown. Place it on top of square A.

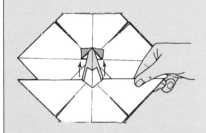

30 Insert the Emperor's head through the hole. Once again, you may have to enlarge the hole slightly first. Arrange the squares so they lie neatly on top of each other.

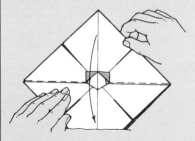

31 Treating the squares as if they were one, valley fold them in half (but not the head) from top to bottom.

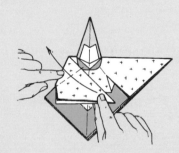

32 Valley fold the left-hand point down as shown.

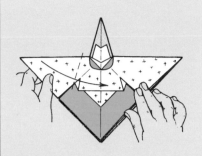

33 Valley fold the point back up as shown.

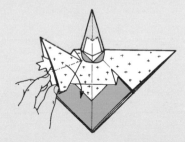

34 Open out the point and squash it down neatly towards the lap, thereby making the Emperor's right shoulder and sleeve.

35   Repeat steps 32 to 34 with the right-hand point, thereby . . .

36   making the Emperor's left shoulder and sleeve.

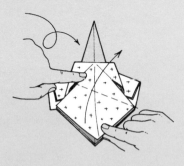

37   Turn the model over. Valley fold the topmost layer of paper up and across to the right.

38   On either side, mountain fold the lower corners up inside the model.

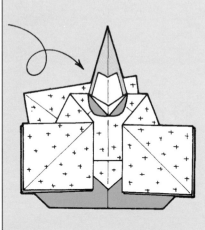

39   Turn the model over to complete the Emperor.

Empress

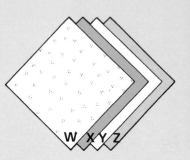

40   As a help during assembly, label the squares with a pencil as follows: patterned W, coloured X, white Y and black Z. Repeat steps 1 to 4.

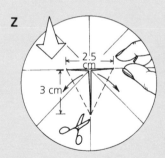

41   To make the various collars, cut each square as shown. Square Z: Repeat steps 5 and 6, but make a T-shaped cut with a width of 2.5 cm (1 inch) and a length of 3 cm (1¼ inches).

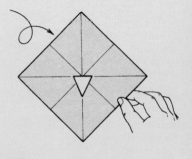

42   Turn square Z over.

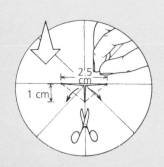

43 Square Y: Repeat steps 5 and 6, but make a T-shaped cut with a width of 2.5 cm (1 inch) and a length of 1 cm (½ inch).

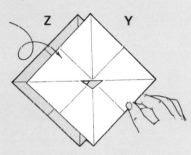

44 Turn square Y over and place it on top of square Z.

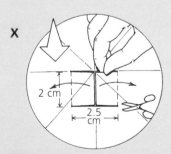

45 Square X: In the square's middle and along its diagonal fold-lines, make an I-shaped cut, with a width of 2.5 cm (1 inch) and a length of 2 cm (¾ inch). Valley fold the middle flaps over, on a line between the top and bottom of the I's 'arms', as shown.

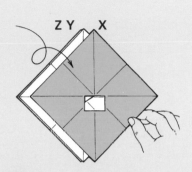

46 Turn square X over and place it on top of squares Y and Z.

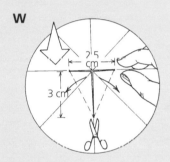

47 Square W: Repeat steps 5 and 6, but make a T-shaped cut with a width of 2.5 cm (1 inch) and a length of 3 cm (1¼ inches).

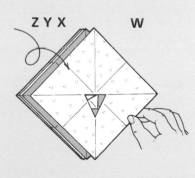

48 Turn square W over and place it on top of squares X, Y and Z.

49 Make sure that the squares are arranged as in step 40. You should now be able to see the various collars.

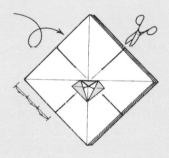

50 Repeat step 15.

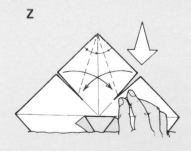

51 Square Z: Repeat steps 16 and 17.

52 Turn square Z over. In the point's topmost layer, make an M-shaped cut, as shown.

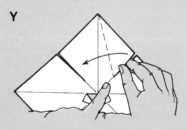

53 Square Y: Repeat steps 19 to 22.

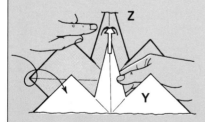

54 Turn square Y over and insert its point into the M-shaped cut of square Z's point. Push the point up inside as far as it will go, thereby making the Empress's head. Now repeat steps 24 to 26.

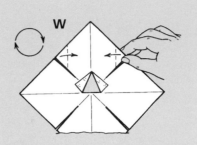

55 Square W: Turn the paper around into the position shown. Valley fold the side corners of the top section in, so that they both make a vertical edge.

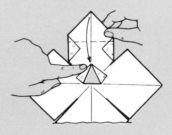

56 Valley fold the top point down to meet the hole.

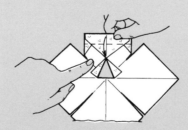

57 Repeat step 56 with the top edge.

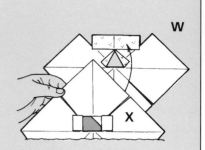

58 Square X: Turn the paper around into the position shown. Place it on top of square W.

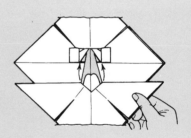

59 Repeat steps 30 to 36.

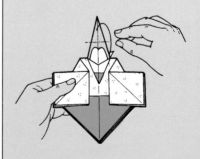

60 Shape the top of the Empress's head with a mountain fold.

61 Turn the model over. Step fold the topmost layer of paper as shown.

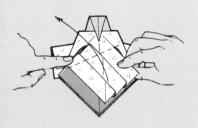

62 Valley fold the topmost layer of paper up and across to the left.

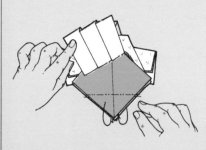

63 Repeat step 38.

64 Turn the model over to complete the Empress.

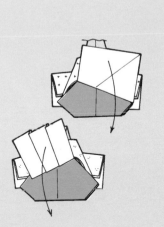

65 Fold the Emperor's and Empress's topmost layers of paper down slightly, so that they will be able to stand.

66 When displaying the dolls, make sure to place the Emperor on your left-hand side and the Empress on your right-hand side, as shown.

TATO HANAMON ORI

(TRADITIONAL)
INTRODUCED BY
MEGUMI BIDDLE

This traditional type of Japanese folded purse makes an ideal container for the Hina Ningyo (see page 98). Tato often take on the form of hexagonal or octagonal stylized flower patterns.

USE TWO SQUARES OF PAPER, IDENTICAL IN SIZE, WHITE SIDE UP. YOU WILL ALSO NEED A PAIR OF SCISSORS.

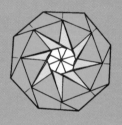

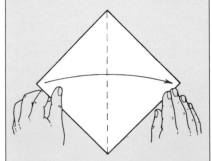

1 Turn one square around to look like a diamond. Valley fold it in half from left to right, thereby making a triangle.

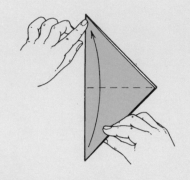

2 Valley fold the triangle in half from bottom to top.

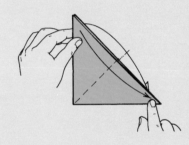

3 Valley fold the triangle's top left-hand point down to meet the bottom right-hand point. Repeat behind.

4 Valley fold the triangle's top left-hand sloping side over to lie along the bottom edge. Repeat behind.

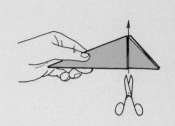

5 Cut along the side of the vertical edge, as shown. Discard the small right-hand triangular piece of paper.

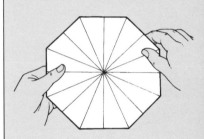

6 Open out the remaining triangle into an octagon. Repeat steps 1 to 6 with the remaining square.

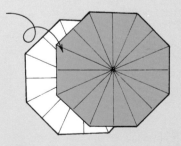

7 Turn the octagons over. Place them together, with their white sides innermost.

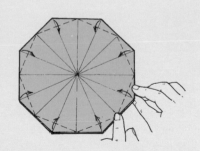

8 Treating the octagons as if they were one, valley fold the eight corners over as shown.

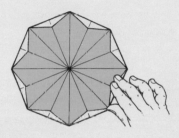

9 This should be the result.

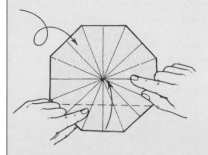

10 Turn the paper over. Valley fold the bottom edge over to meet the middle, thereby making a flap of paper.

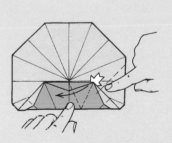

11 Open out the flap's right-hand side and at the same time . . .

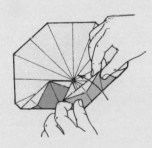

12 swing the adjacent edge of the octagon over to meet the middle. Press the paper flat into the position shown in step 13.

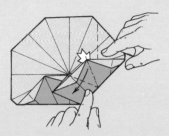

13 Repeat steps 11 and 12, continuing anti-clockwise around the model. Most of the creases shown already exist; some will have to be formed.

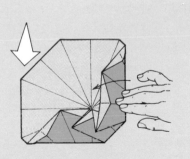

14 Following the illustration, carefully swing this edge over to meet the middle.

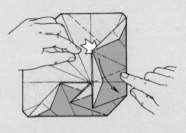

15 Remember to fold carefully as you open out this flap's right-hand side.

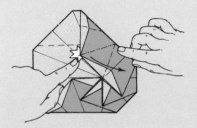

16 You are now halfway to completion.

17 With a little patience, open out this flap, as shown.

18 Don't give up hope - you're nearly there!

19 Open out the penultimate flap, while at the same time . . .

20 pulling out the remaining flap of paper. Press the paper flat into the position shown in step 21.

21 Valley fold the remaining flap's right-hand side over on a line between its bottom left-hand corner and the octagon's middle. Press the paper flat, thereby . . .

22 completing the tato.

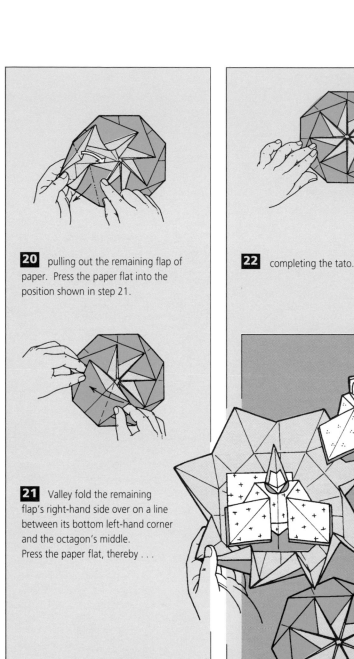

23 To open the tato, pull opposite flaps apart; release them and it will return to its original form.

Variation 1

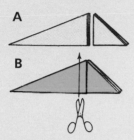

1 Repeat steps 1 to 4 of the tato on page 106 with each square. Label the triangles A and B. Cut along the vertical edge of triangle A. Discard the small right-hand triangular piece of paper. Cut triangle B as shown. Discard the right-hand piece of paper.

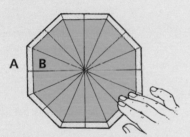

2 Open out triangles A and B into octagons. Place the octagons together as shown, with their coloured sides on top.

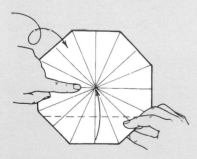

3 Treating the octagons as if they were one, repeat steps 10 to 22 of the tato on pages 107 to 108.

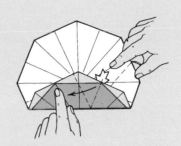

4 Here is the completed variation 1.

Variation 2

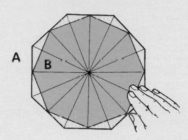

5 Repeat steps 1 to 6 of the tato on page 106 with each square. Place the octagons together as shown, with their coloured sides on top.

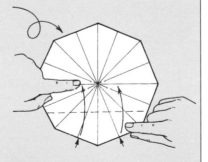

6 Treating the octagons as if they were one, turn them over and around, into the position shown. Valley fold the bottom point up, so that the fold-lines on either side and the adjacent underneath horizontal edge meet the middle, thereby making a flap.

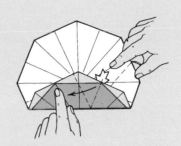

7 Open out the flap's right-hand side, at the same time . . .

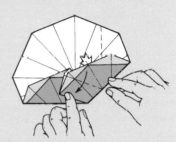

8 swinging the adjacent underneath horizontal edge over to lie along the middle. Continue repeating steps 7 and 8 anti-clockwise around the model. Most of the creases shown already exist; some will have to be formed. In effect, repeat steps 14 to 22 of the tato on pages 107 to 108.

9 Here is the completed variation 2.

SYMMETRY AND BEAUTY

Origami procedures such as multiple sinking, pleating and petal folding, are perhaps the most advanced of all origami techniques, but with the correct preparation and practice they are no more difficult than other techniques. Multiple sinking takes many guises, and it can be used to produce a variety of symmetrical forms. By pleating the paper, and by stretching or spreading the pleats, it is possible to transform the paper into a beautiful star or frill. Petal folding is employed in the making of the traditional bird base. This base is thought by many paperfolders to be the keystone to origami.

As we have already said, many paperfolders like to fold models on a single theme. Francis Ow, for example, a well-known Singapore origami artist, specializes in folding origami hearts, of which two are featured in this chapter.

PENCIL AND PAPER

MEGUMI BIDDLE

This model makes an ideal decoration for a piece of notepaper or personal stationery. It is based upon a model that was originally created by Takenao Handa.

USE A SQUARE OF PAPER, WHITE SIDE UP.

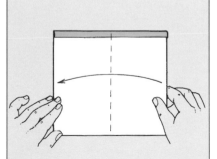

2 Valley fold the paper in half from right to left.

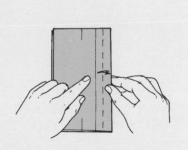

5 Valley fold the right-hand side over to meet the fold-line made in step 4. Press it flat and unfold it.

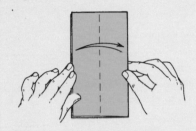

3 Again, valley fold the paper in half from right to left, but do not press the paper completely flat. Press down on it only a little, at the top and bottom points, then unfold it.

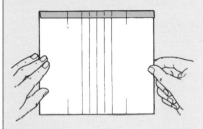

6 Open out the paper from left to right.

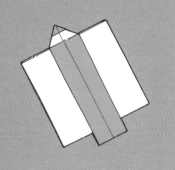

1 Valley fold down a little of the top edge.

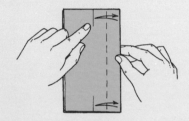

4 Valley fold the right-hand side over to meet the fold-marks made in step 3. Press it flat and unfold it.

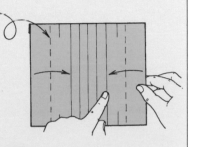

7 Turn the paper over. Valley fold the sides over to meet the fold-lines made in step 4.

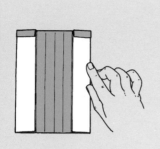

8 This should be the result.

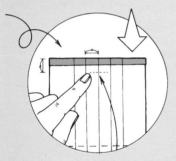

9 Turn the paper over. Valley fold the bottom edge up as far as shown.

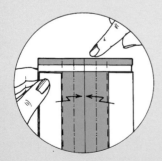

10 Along the fold-lines made in steps 4 and 5, step fold the middle section of paper. You will have to reverse some of the fold-lines.

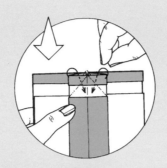

11 Inside reverse fold the middle section's top corners, thereby making the pencil.

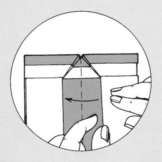

12 Valley fold the pencil in half from right to left.

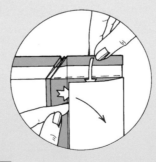

13 Valley fold the right-hand half of the top edge down, at the same time . . .

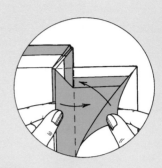

14 inserting it underneath the adjacent layer of paper. Valley fold the pencil's top layer back over.

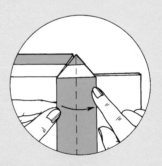

15 Valley fold the pencil in half from left to right. Repeat steps 13 to 14 with the left-hand half of the top edge.

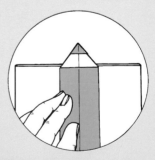

16 This should be the result.

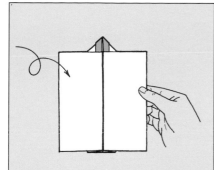

17 Turn the model over.

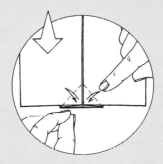

18 Valley fold the middle corners over, so that they lie along the underneath vertical edges. Press them flat and unfold them.

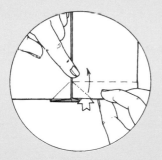

19 Valley fold the right-hand half of the bottom edge up, so that the adjacent middle corner rises up.

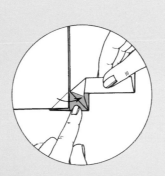

20 Along the fold-lines made in step 18, squash the corner's folded edge down.

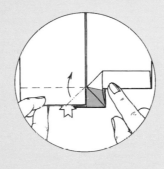

21 Repeat steps 19 to 21 with the left-hand half of the bottom edge.

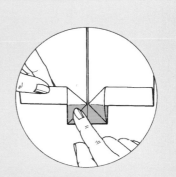

22 This should be the result.

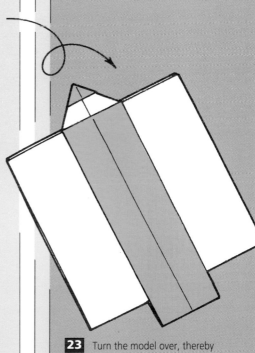

23 Turn the model over, thereby completing the pencil and paper.

DISH

DIDIER BOURSIN

Didier Boursin specializes in creating models that have a clean and elegant line, of which this dish is a perfect example.

USE A SQUARE OF PAPER, WHITE SIDE UP.

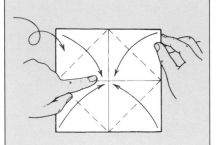

2 Turn the paper over. Valley fold the corners into the middle, thereby . . .

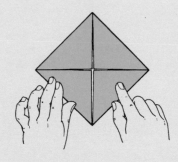

3 making a blintz base.

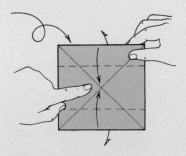

4 Turn the blintz base over and around, into the position shown. Valley fold the top and bottom edges over to meet the middle fold-line, at the same time . . .

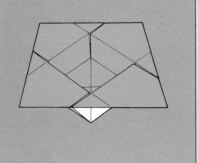

1 Valley fold the opposite sides and top and bottom edges together in turn to mark the vertical and horizontal fold-lines, then open up again.

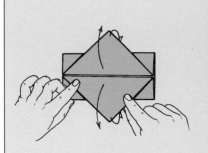

5 letting the corners from underneath flick up. Press the paper flat. Return the top and bottom edges to their original positions.

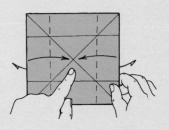

6 Valley fold the sides over to meet the middle fold-line, at the same time . . .

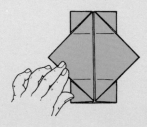

7 letting the corners from underneath flick up. Press the paper flat.

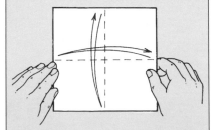

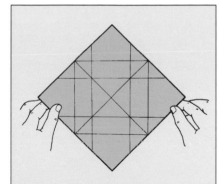

8 Unfold the paper completely.

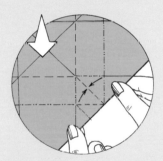

9 Working on one sloping edge and using the existing valley and mountain fold-lines . . .

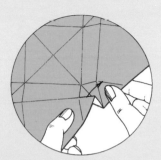

10 form one side of the dish. In step 9 most of the creases shown already exist; only the lower sloping mountain fold will have to be formed, thereby making a small triangular flap.

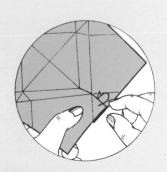

11 Mountain fold the triangular flap down . . .

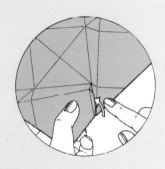

12 inside the model, thereby locking all the folds together.

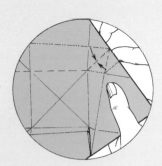

13 Repeat steps 9, 10, . . .

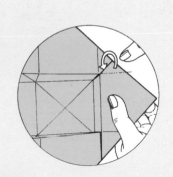

14 11 and 12 anti-clockwise around the model, thereby forming the dish's remaining three sides.

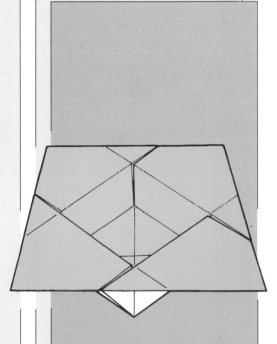

15 Here is the completed dish.

ON THE WINGS OF LOVE

F R A N C I S   O W

This model is carrying a hidden message, perhaps a message of love.

USE A SQUARE OF PAPER, WHITE SIDE UP.

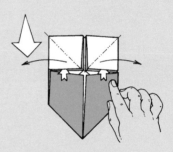

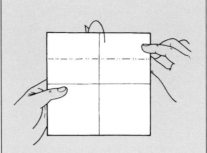

2 Mountain fold the top edge behind to meet the middle fold-line.

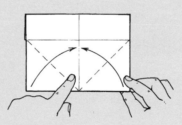

3 Valley fold the bottom corners up to meet the middle fold-line, thereby making a shape that looks like an upside-down roof.

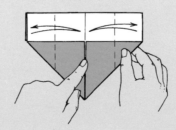

4 Valley fold the sides in to meet the middle fold-line. Press them flat and unfold them.

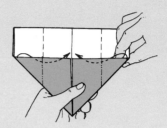

5 Using the fold-lines made in step 4 as a guide, inside reverse fold the sides into the upside-down roof as shown.

6 Open out the upper right-hand layers of paper and pull the top layer over as shown. Squash the paper down neatly into the shape of a triangle. Repeat this step with the upper left-hand layers of paper.

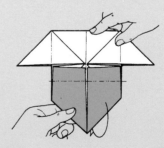

7 Mountain fold the bottom point behind to meet the top edge, so that . . .

1 Valley fold the opposite sides and top and bottom edges together in turn to mark the vertical and horizontal fold-lines, then open up again.

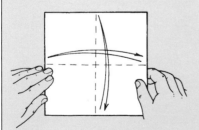

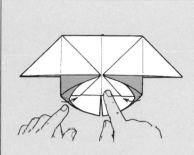

8 the inside layers rise up. Press them flat into the position shown in step 9.

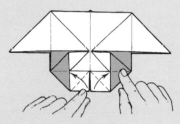

9 Valley fold the middle corners over to meet their adjacent vertical edges.

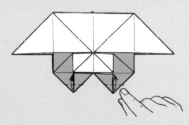

10 Valley fold the bottom points up to meet the adjacent horizontal edge.

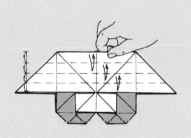

11 Divide the roof-like section of paper into quarters by valley folding. Press it flat and unfold it.

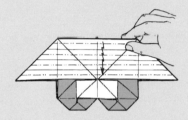

12 Pleat the roof-like section of paper into eight by mountain and valley folding as shown. Note that the valley folds take place along existing fold-lines.

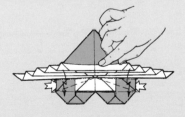

13 Step fold the pleats' adjacent layers of paper as shown, thereby . . .

14 forming the wings. Spread them out a little.

15 To complete, turn the model over.

DOUBLE HEARTS

FRANCIS OW

As this model is flat, it can be contained in an envelope together with your love letters or greetings cards.

USE A RECTANGLE OF PAPER, 2 X 1 IN PROPORTION, WHITE SIDE UP.

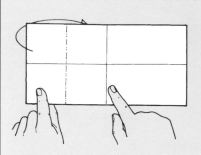

2   Mountain fold the left-hand side behind to meet the middle fold-line.

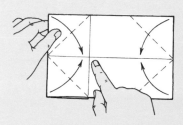

3   Valley fold the corners over to meet the horizontal middle fold-line, thereby making roof-like shapes at each end.

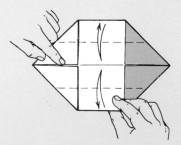

4   Valley fold the top and bottom edges over to meet the middle fold-line. Press them flat and unfold them.

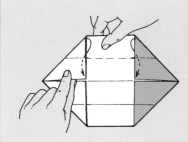

5   Using the fold-lines made in step 4 as a guide, and treating the left-hand layers of paper as if they were one, inside reverse fold the top edge into the adjacent 'roofs'.

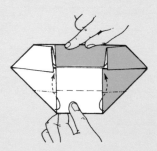

6   Repeat step 5 with the bottom edge.

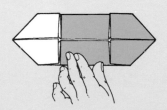

7   This should be the result.

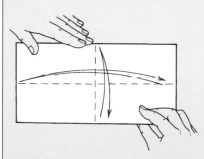

1   Place the rectangle sideways on. Valley fold the opposite sides and top and bottom edges together in turn to mark the vertical and horizontal fold-lines, then open up again.

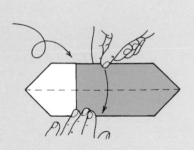

8 Turn the paper over. Valley fold it in half from top to bottom.

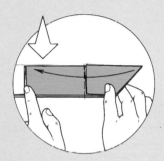

9 Valley fold the right-hand point over to meet the left-hand vertical edge.

10 Lift the right-hand point up. Open out the point and . . .

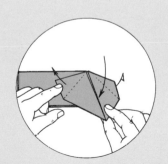

11 squash it down neatly . . .

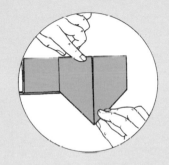

12 into a heart-like shape, as shown.

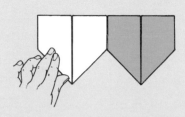

13 Repeat steps 10 to 12 with the left-hand point.

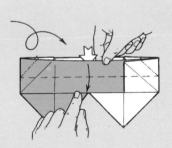

14 Turn the paper over. Valley fold the front top edges (but not the middle section of paper) down to meet the horizontal folded edge, so that the top corners rise up. Squash them down flat.

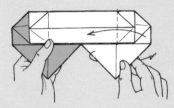

15 Swing the right-hand heart around to the front.

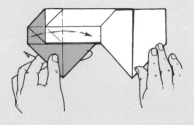

16 Repeat step 15 with the left-hand heart.

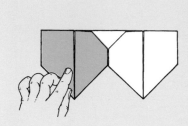

17 This should be the result.

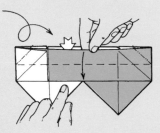

18 Repeat step 14.

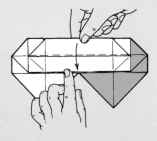

19 Valley fold the middle section of paper down to meet the horizontal folded edge, thereby making a bridge.

20 Valley fold each heart's middle corners over to meet their adjacent horizontal edges.

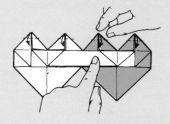

21 Valley fold each heart's top points down a little.

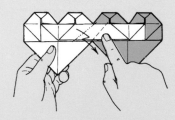

22 Step fold the bridge to adjust the position . . .

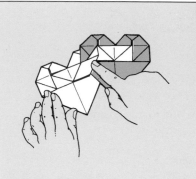

23 of the hearts.

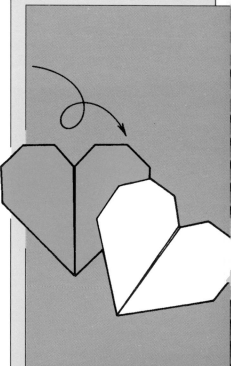

24 To complete, turn the hearts over.

STAR

MEGUMI BIDDLE

This model looks most beautiful made out of shiny metallic foil (the kind that is used for gift wrapping).

USE A SQUARE OF PAPER, WHITE SIDE UP.

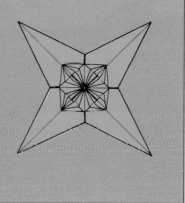

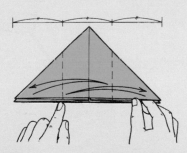

1 Begin with a waterbomb base (see page 26, steps 1 to 6). Valley fold the top right-hand flap of paper over to a point two-thirds of the distance to the opposite side. Press it flat and unfold it. Repeat this step with the top left-hand flap.

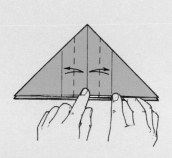

2 Valley fold the fold-lines made in step 1 over to meet the middle fold-line. Press them flat and unfold them.

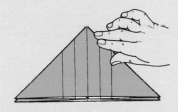

3 This should be the result.

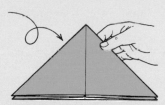

4 Turn the paper over. Repeat steps 1 and 2 with the top right- and left-hand flaps of paper.

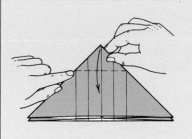

5 Valley fold the top point down on a line between the fold-lines made in step 1.

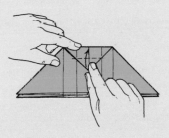

6 Valley fold the point back up to meet the middle of the top edge.

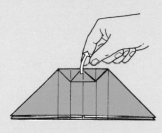

7 This should be the result. Press the point flat and unfold it.

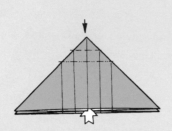

8   Double sink the top point. This is what you do:

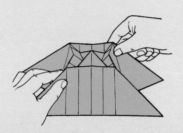

9   Repeat step 3 of the sink on page 15, creasing along the fold-lines made in step 5. Pinch the inner square at opposite corners and, working towards the middle, make the point rise up along the fold-lines made in step 6. Finally, collapse the paper into the position shown in step 10.

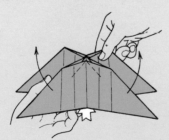

10   Open out the model from the inside, thereby . . .

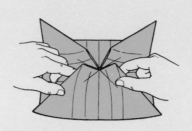

11   making the four flaps rise up.

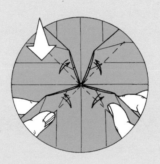

12   Valley fold the flaps over to meet the middle fold-lines. Press them flat and unfold them.

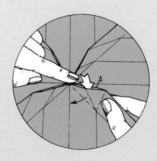

13   Open out one flap and . . .

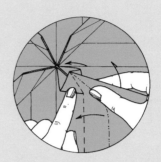

14   squash it down into the middle, as shown, thereby making its adjacent corner rise up.

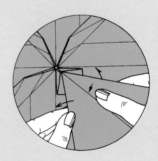

15   Along the fold-lines made in steps 1 and 2, open out and squash down the corner.

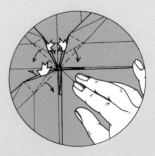

16   This should be the result. Repeat steps 13 to 15 with the remaining three flaps.

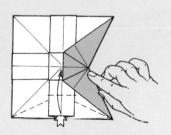

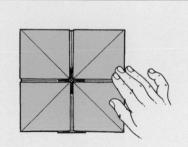

17 This should be the result.

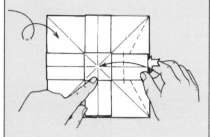

18 Turn the model over. Valley fold one 'pleated' section of paper over to meet the middle, thereby . . .

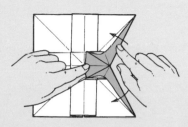

19 making the adjacent edges rise up. Flatten the edges down . . .

20 to form squash folds, as shown. Without turning the model over, repeat steps 18 to 20, working clockwise around the model.

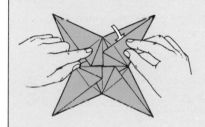

21 Arrange the flattened edges to fit one over the other.

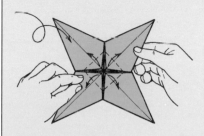

22 Turn the model over. Valley fold the four middle points out, thereby . . .

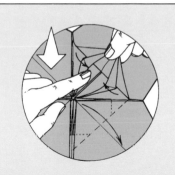

23 making their underneath layers of paper rise up.

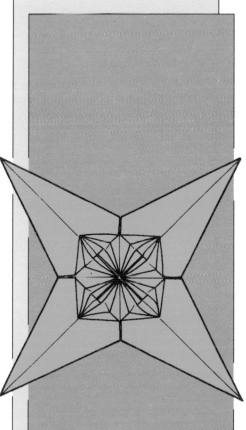

24 Here is the completed star.

ROSE BROOCH

TOSHIE TAKAHAMA

Have fun folding this model, as you will learn how to fold a very important origami base.

USE A SQUARE OF PAPER, WHITE SIDE UP.

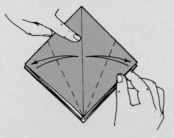

1 Begin with a preliminary fold (see page 80, steps 1 to 6). Valley fold the lower (open) sloping edges over, so they lie along the middle fold-line. Press them flat and unfold them.

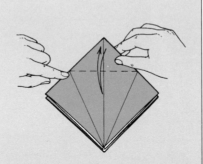

2 Valley fold the top point down on a line between the fold-lines made in step 1. Press it flat and unfold it. Now make a petal fold. This is what you do:

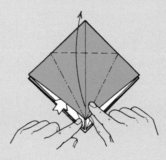

3 Pinch and lift up the front flap of paper.

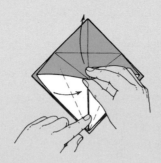

4 Continue to lift up the front flap of paper, so . . .

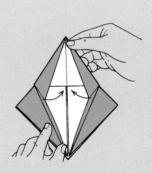

5 that its edges meet in the middle.

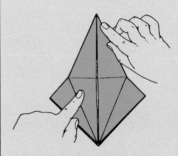

6 Press the paper flat, thereby making it diamond-shaped. This completes the petal fold.

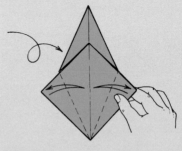

7 Turn the paper over. Valley fold the lower (open) sloping edges over, so they lie along the middle fold-line. Press them flat and unfold them. Repeat steps 2 to 6, thereby . . .

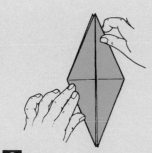

8 making a very important shape that in origami is called the bird base. (The bird base comes in two forms, either as shown here, or with its top flaps valley folded down in front and behind.)

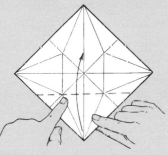

9 Open out the bird base completely, with the white side on top. Valley fold the bottom point up along a line that uses the intersection of the lower fold-lines as its location point.

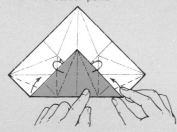

10 The following folds take place along existing fold-lines. Mountain fold the point's sloping edges behind to lie along the vertical middle fold-line, at the same time letting the lower right- and left-hand sloping edges swing up to meet the horizontal middle fold-line. Press the paper flat, thereby making a point.

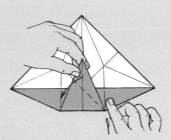

11 Valley fold the point over towards the left.

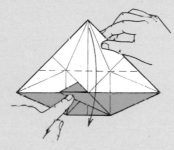

12 Valley fold the top point down along a line that uses the intersection of the upper fold-lines as its location point.

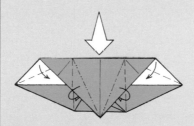

13 Repeat step 10 with the top point, at the same time letting the upper right- and left-hand sloping edges swing down to meet the horizontal middle fold-line.

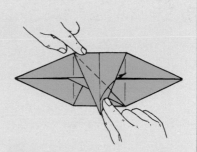

14 Valley fold the point over towards the right.

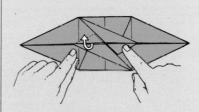

15 Release the point from underneath the top layer of paper.

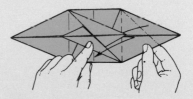

16 Step fold the right-hand point as shown, at the same time inserting it underneath the adjacent point.

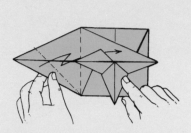

17 Step fold the left-hand point as shown, at the same time inserting it underneath the adjacent point.

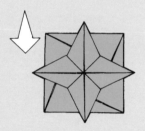

18 This should be the result.

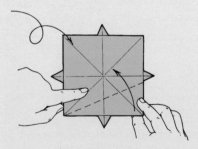

19 Turn the model over. From the bottom left-hand corner, valley fold the bottom edge up to meet the diagonal fold-line.

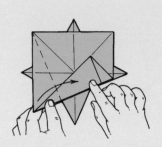

20 From the top left-hand corner, valley fold the left-hand side over to meet the diagonal fold-line.

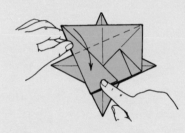

21 From the top right-hand corner, valley fold the top edge down to meet the diagonal fold-line.

22 Inside reverse fold the right-hand side as shown, thereby making an 'inner' diamond.

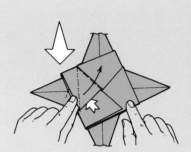

23 Valley fold the diamond's lower left-hand side point across as shown, at the same time letting the paper arrange itself into a sort of petal fold.

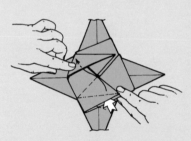

24 Repeat step 23 with the diamond's lower right-hand side point, at the same time inserting it underneath the previous one.

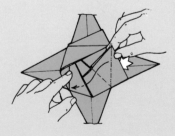

25 Repeat step 24 with the diamond's upper right-hand side point.

26 Finally, repeat step 24 with the diamond's upper left-hand side point. Make sure that the points are arranged as shown.

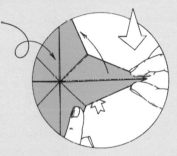

27 Turn the model over. Pinch the right-hand point and fold it over as shown. This is a leaf.

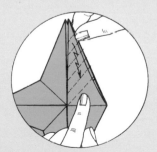

28 Make a series of valley and mountain folds along the leaf as shown.

29 Open out and squash down the leaf, but being careful not to flatten completely . . .

30 the folds made in step 28.

31 Without turning the model over, repeat steps 27 to 30 with the top point.

32 Repeat step 31 with the left hand point and bottom point.

33 Turn the model over. Open out its centre a little, thereby completing the rose brooch.

SINK FLOWER

STEVE BIDDLE

Making this model is a very good lesson in the technique of double sinking.

USE A SQUARE OF PAPER, WHITE SIDE UP.

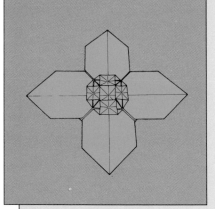

1 Begin with a preliminary fold (see page 80, steps 1 to 6). Valley fold the front flap of paper in half from bottom to top, being careful to mark only the middle point. Unfold it. Repeat behind.

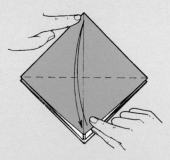

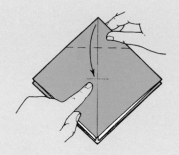

2 Valley fold the top point down to where the fold-lines intersect.

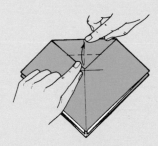

3 Valley fold the point back up to meet the middle of the top edge.

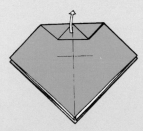

4 This should be the result. Press the point flat and unfold it.

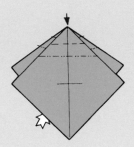

5 Double sink the top point. This is what you do:

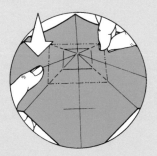

6 Repeat step 3 of the sink on page 15, creasing along the fold-lines made in step 2.

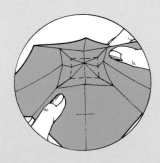

7 Pinch the inner square at opposite corners and, working towards the middle, . . .

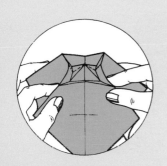

8 make the middle point rise up along the fold-lines made in step 3. Finally, . . .

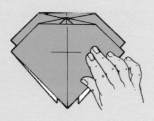

9 collapse the paper into the position shown.

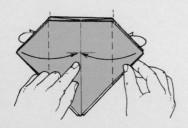

10 Valley fold the side points over to where the fold-lines intersect. Repeat behind.

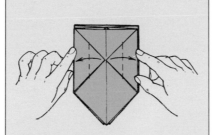

11 Valley fold the side points back out to meet the middle of their adjacent sides. Repeat behind.

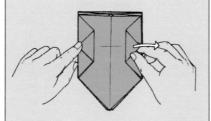

12 This should be the result. Press the side points flat. Unfold the right-hand side point.

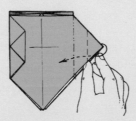

13 Double reverse fold the right-hand side point. This is what you do: using the fold-line made in step 10 as a guide, inside reverse fold the point into the model.

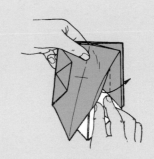

14 Using the fold-line made in step 11 as a guide, reverse fold the point back out.

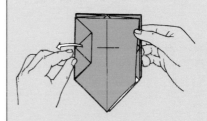

15 Unfold the left-hand side point.

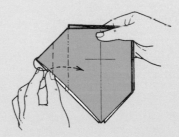

16 Repeat steps 13 and 14 with the left-hand side point. Turn the model over. Repeat steps 12 to 16.

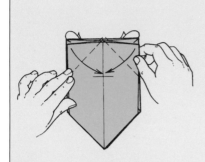

17 Valley fold the top points down to meet the vertical fold-line. Repeat behind.

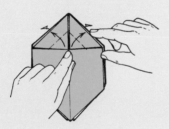

18 Valley fold the top points back out to meet the middle of their adjacent sloping edges. Repeat behind.

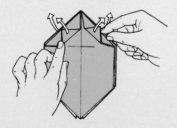

19 This should be the result. Press the points flat and unfold them.

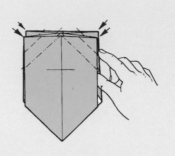

20 Along the fold-lines made in steps 17 and 18, double sink the four top points.

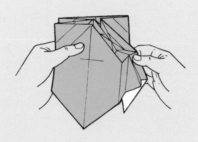

21 This shows step 20 taking place.

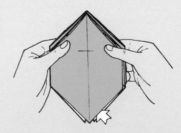

22 This should be the result. Open out the model from the inside, thereby . . .

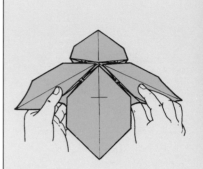

23 making the four flaps rise up.

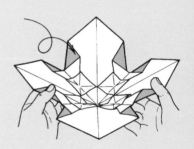

24 Turn the model over.

25 Carefully press the model flat, as shown.

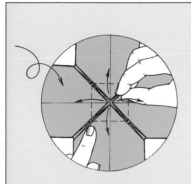

26 Turn the model over. Valley fold the four middle points out.

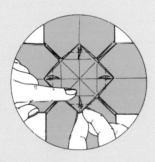

27 Valley fold the middle points in, as shown. Press them flat and unfold them.

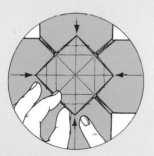

28 Along the fold-lines made in step 27, sink each middle point.

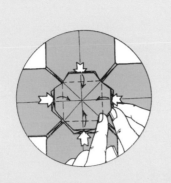

29 Open out each of the four sinks, . . .

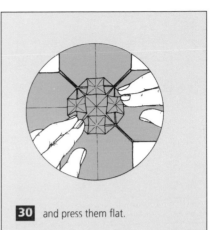

30 and press them flat.

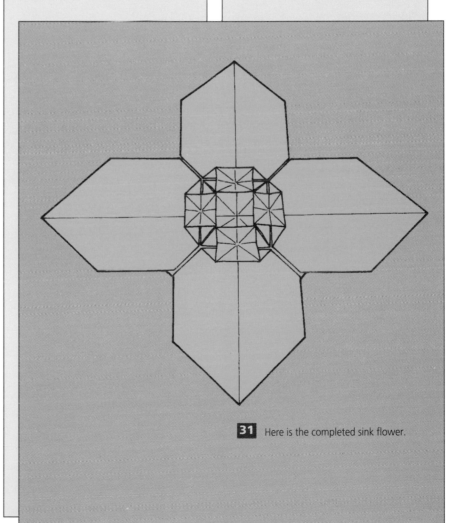

31 Here is the completed sink flower.

PIERROT

SEIJI NISHIKAWA

This is one of the most complicated pieces of origami in this book, so take your time and make your folds carefully.

USE TWO SQUARES OF PAPER, IDENTICAL IN SIZE. YOU WILL ALSO NEED A TUBE OF PAPER GLUE.

The Face

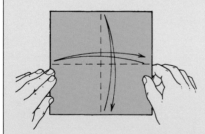

1 Place one square of paper coloured side up and valley fold the opposite sides and top and bottom edges together in turn to mark the vertical and horizontal fold-lines, then open up again.

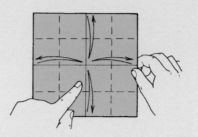

2 Valley fold the opposite sides and top and bottom edges to the middle in turn to mark the quarter fold-lines, then open up again.

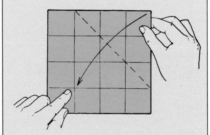

3 Valley fold the top right-hand corner over to where the lower left-hand quarter fold-lines intersect.

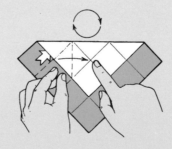

4 Turn the paper around, into the position shown. Along the existing fold-lines, lift up, . . .

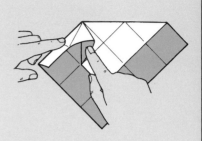

5 open out and squash the left-hand side of the top flap down.

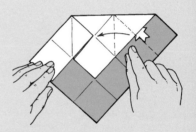

6 With the paper in the same position, repeat steps 4 and 5 with the right-hand side of the top flap, thereby making a flap of paper appear in the centre of the model.

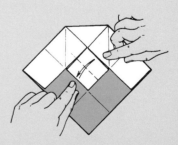

7 Valley fold the flap in half from bottom left to top right. Press it flat and unfold it.

8 This shows step 7 taking place.

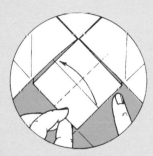

9 Valley fold the flap in half from bottom right to top left, then . . .

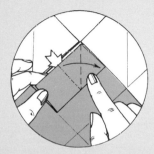

10 fold it towards the right, making the vertical valley fold as shown, at the same time . . .

11 pushing the bottom left-hand edge up along the valley fold-line made in step 7. Press the paper flat into a small triangular flap that points towards the right.

12 Open out and squash the triangular flap down neatly into an upside-down preliminary fold. This is the start of the pierrot's nose.

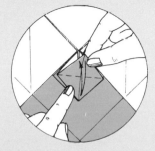

13 Valley fold the nose's front flap of paper in half from top to bottom. Press it flat and unfold it.

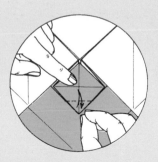

14 Valley fold the nose's bottom point up to meet the fold-line made in step 13. Press it flat and unfold it, thereby preparing the paper for a sink.

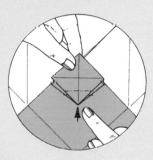

15 Along the fold-lines made in step 14, . . .

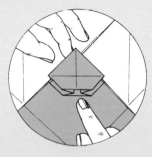

16 sink (see page 15, steps 1 to 5) the nose's bottom point.

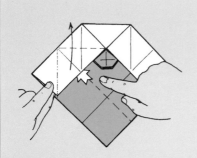

17 This step looks more tricky than it is. Insert your forefinger underneath the left-hand sloping layer of paper and open it up along the horizontal valley fold-line as shown, at the same time . . .

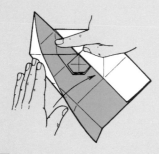

18 pushing the lower left-hand edge up to lie along the right-hand sloping layer of paper. Press the paper flat.

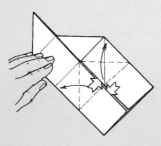

19 Reach inside and open the right-hand layers of paper out.

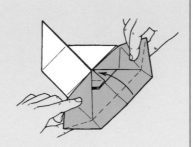

20 Pull the layers apart and press them flat into the position shown.

21 Open out and squash the bottom triangular point down neatly . . .

22 into an upside-down preliminary fold.

23 Petal fold the preliminary fold's front flap of paper (see page 124, steps 1 to 6).

24 Reach inside the petal fold and pull out the nose.

25 On the petal fold, make the valley folds as shown, thereby opening it out, at the same time . . .

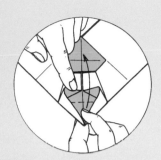

26 lifting up the petal fold's bottom point, as shown. Press the paper flat.

27 This should be the result. Valley fold what was originally the petal fold's bottom point down along the nose's horizontal fold line. This is the start of the pierrot's mouth.

28 Valley fold the sides of the mouth down as shown, thereby creating two small triangles on either side.

29 Valley fold the mouth down on a line between the tops of the two triangles. You will have to adjust the position of the triangles slightly so this fold can be made.

30 Shape the pierrot's chin with a mountain fold.

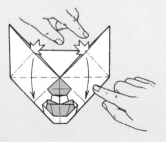

31 Open out and squash the top triangular points down neatly into sideways-on preliminary folds.

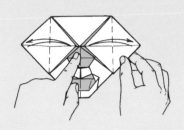

32 Valley fold the right- and left-hand side points into the middle. Press them flat and unfold them.

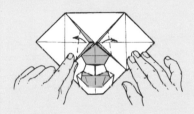

33 Valley fold the front flap of each preliminary fold over on a slant, thereby suggesting the eyes. (You can make the pierrot look happy or sad by changing the angle of these folds.)

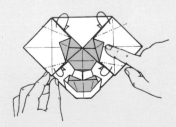

34 Mountain fold the top and bottom points of each preliminary fold . . .

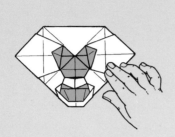

35 behind on a slant.

36 Shape the sides of the nose with mountain folds.

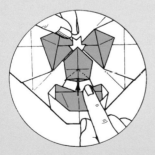

37 Push and pinch the bottom of the nose in, at the same time . . .

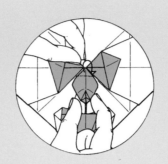

38 shaping the top of the nose with a mountain fold, making it become three-dimensional.

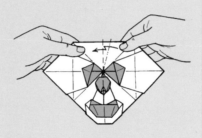

39 Step fold the forehead as shown, thereby making the face become convex.

40 On one side of the forehead, make a mountain fold on a line between the side point and the middle of the top of the head. Repeat on the other side. These final mountain folds will hold the folds made in step 39 in place, thereby completing the pierrot's face.

Frill and Hair

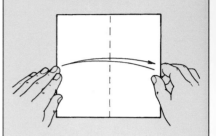

41 Place the remaining square white side up and valley fold it in half from side to side. Press it flat and unfold it.

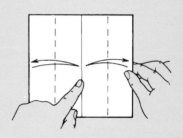

42 Valley fold the sides over to meet the middle fold-line. Press them flat and unfold them.

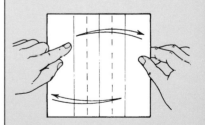

43 Valley fold the sides over as shown. Press them flat and unfold them.

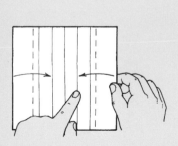

44 Valley fold the left-hand side over to meet the left-hand fold-line made in step 43, thereby making a panel of paper. Repeat with the right-hand side.

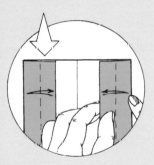

45 Valley fold the panels in half from side to side. Press them flat and unfold them.

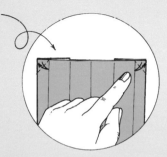

46 Turn the paper over. Valley fold the top corners down to meet their adjacent fold-lines. Press them flat and unfold them.

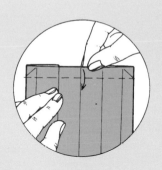

47 Valley fold the top edge down at the bottom of the fold-lines made in step 46.

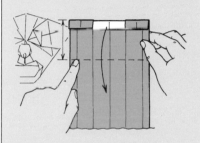

48 Using the length of the pierrot's face as a guide to the position of this fold-line, valley fold the top edge down as shown.

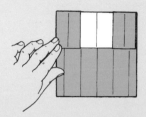

49 This should be the result.

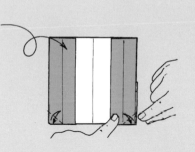

50 Turn the paper over from top to bottom. Valley fold the bottom corners up to meet their adjacent fold-lines. Press them flat and unfold them.

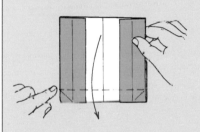

51 Valley fold the front flap of paper down at the top of the fold-lines made in step 50, thereby . . .

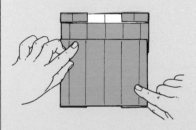

52 making a pleat in the paper.

138

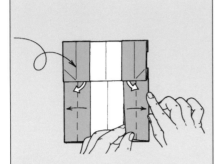

53 Turn the paper over. Valley fold the lower right-hand panel in half from side to side, at the same time . . .

54 pulling the concealed paper out from underneath the pleat.

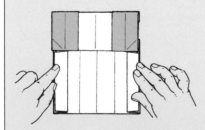

55 With the paper in the same position, repeat steps 53 and 54 with the lower left-hand panel. This should be the result.

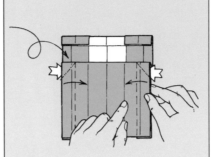

56 Turn the paper over. Valley fold the sides over to meet their adjacent fold-lines, at the same time squashing down the pleat neatly into the position shown in step 57.

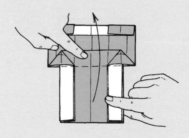

57 Valley fold the bottom edge up along the line of the horizontal edge behind.

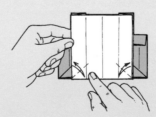

58 Valley fold the right- and left-hand sides of the top flap over to lie along the bottom edge; only pressing down on the fold where marked by the lines of dashes.

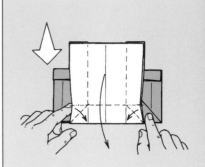

59 Valley fold the top flap's sides in . . .

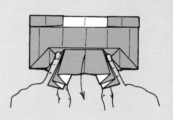

60 and down as shown, thereby making a rectangular flap of paper.

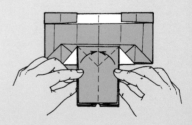

61 Pinch together the two sides of the rectangular flap and . . .

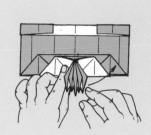

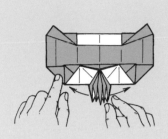

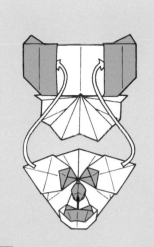

62 lay it down, so that it points to the right, thereby performing an origami technique known as a rabbit's ear.

65 Open the rectangular flap out and . . .

68 Insert the pierrot's face underneath the panels as shown.

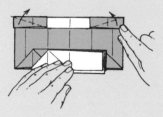

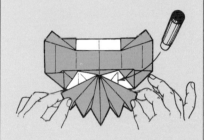

63 Valley fold the top flap's corners up as shown.

66 glue each end on to the pleat as shown, thereby making the frill.

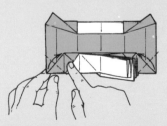

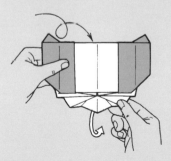

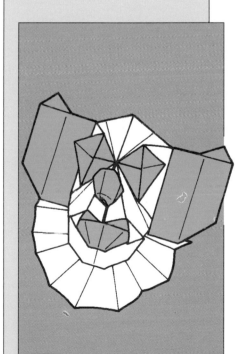

64 Valley fold the bottom corners up to meet the top of the pleat as shown.

67 Turn the model over. Bring the frill around to the front.

69 Here is the completed pierrot.

DELIGHTFUL ANIMALS

Animals can be one of the most challenging subjects to create in the world of origami. However, once the basic shape of an animal is accomplished, slight variations can be introduced to change the angle of the head, ears, legs and tail.

When making your own animal models, study the number of points that the various origami bases have, and the positions of the points within each base, then pick the base that you feel is most suitable for your creation. Alternatively, like many present-day paperfolders, you could try developing new folding bases and techniques to make animal models that look just like the real thing.

TURTLE

(TRADITIONAL)
INTRODUCED BY
TAKENAO HANDA

This model is very popular among Japanese children, but it is comparatively unknown in the West.

USE A SQUARE OF PAPER, WHITE SIDE UP.

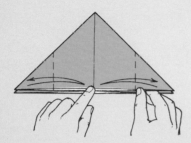

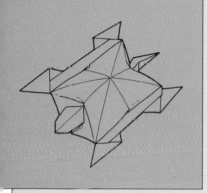

1 Begin with a waterbomb base (see page 26, steps 1 to 6). Valley fold the bottom points over to meet the middle of the bottom edge. Press them flat and unfold them.

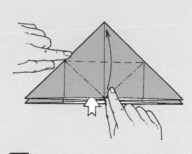

2 Valley fold the top layer of paper in half from bottom to top, thereby making . . .

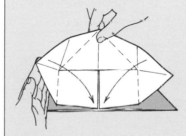

3 the bottom points rise up. Bring the edges of each point to . . .

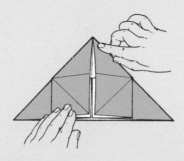

4 the vertical middle line in a fold similar to a petal fold.

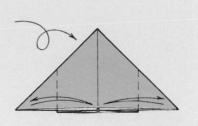

5 Turn the model over. Valley fold the bottom points over to meet the middle of the bottom edge. Press them flat and unfold them. Repeat steps 2 to 4.

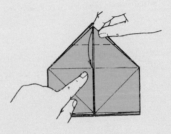

6 Valley fold the top point down into the middle.

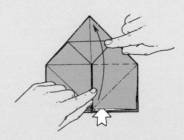

7 Open out the right-hand layer of paper and squash it . . .

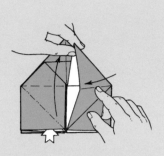

8   down neatly into a triangle. Repeat steps 7 and 8 with the left-hand layer of paper.

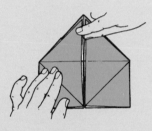

9   This should be the result.

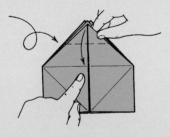

10   Turn the model over. Repeat steps 6 to 9.

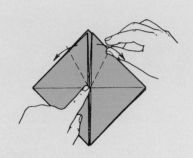

11   Valley fold the top points out . . .

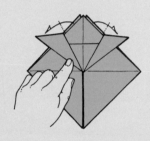

12   from the middle as shown. These are the turtle's legs. Repeat steps 11 and 12 behind.

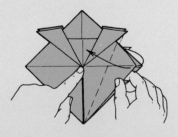

13   From the bottom point, valley fold the right-hand sloping edge over to lie along the vertical middle line. Repeat behind.

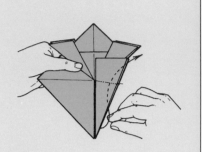

14   Inside reverse fold the bottom right-hand point.

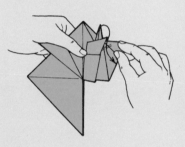

15   Inside reverse fold the right-hand point's tip, to make the tail.

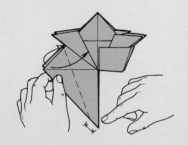

16   Valley fold the left-hand sloping edge over as shown. Repeat behind.

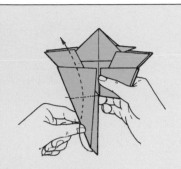

17 Inside reverse fold the bottom left-hand point, thereby . . .

18 making the turtle's neck.

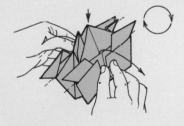

19 Pick up the model and hold it in either hand, as shown. Gently pull the legs apart, at the same time . . .

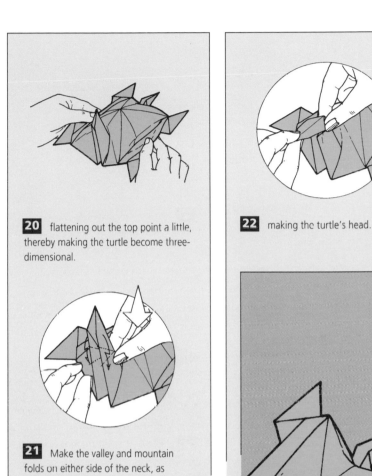

20 flattening out the top point a little, thereby making the turtle become three-dimensional.

21 Make the valley and mountain folds on either side of the neck, as shown, thereby . . .

22 making the turtle's head.

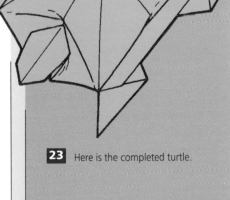

23 Here is the completed turtle.

SYACHI HOKO

KAZUO CHOSHI

Kazuo Choshi's original occupation was coal mining. However, after an accident left him disabled, he developed his interest in origami, and is now teaching paperfolding as an aid to rehabilitation. Most of Kazuo Choshi's models are linked in some way to his home city of Nagoya, Japan. This model is a perfect example; it represents a golden dolphin-like fish that can be found on the roof of Nagoya castle.

USE A SQUARE OF PAPER, WHITE SIDE UP.

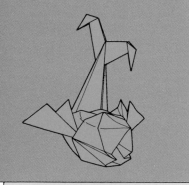

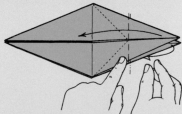

1 Begin with a bird base (see pages 124 to 125, steps 1 to 8). Turn the base around so that its flaps point to the right. Valley fold the front flap over towards the left as shown. Repeat behind.

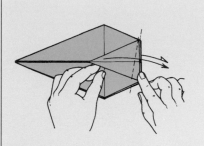

2 Valley fold the front flap out on a slant. Repeat behind.

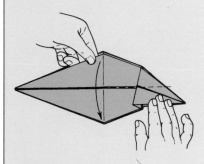

3 Valley fold the top point down to the bottom, as . . .

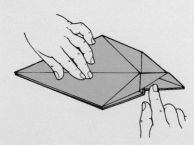

4 though turning the page of a book.

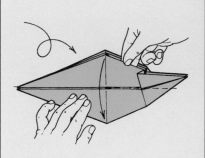

5 Turn the model over from top to bottom. Repeat steps 3 and 4.

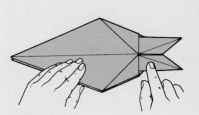

6 This should be the result. The right-hand points are the fish's front fins.

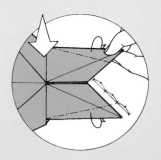

7 Mountain fold the fins as shown.

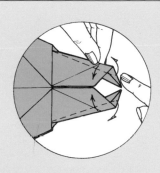

8 Valley fold the fins as shown, at the same time letting the fold made in step 7 come around to the front.

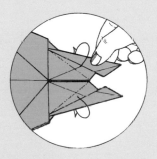

9 Mountain fold each fin behind along the line of its adjacent, underneath sloping edge.

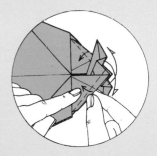

10 Valley fold the fins as shown, at the same time letting them come around to the front.

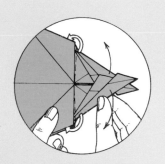

11 Gently swivel the fins apart, thereby rearranging . . .

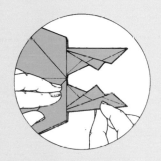

12 their inside adjoining layers of paper. Press them flat.

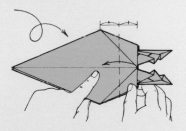

13 Turn the model over. Valley fold the fins over towards the left as shown.

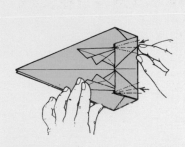

14 Shape the fish's gills with valley and mountain folds.

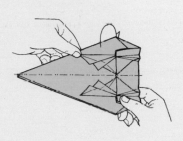

15 Mountain fold the model in half from top to bottom.

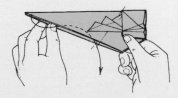

16 Treating the left-hand points as if they were one, inside reverse fold them downwards.

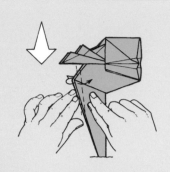

17 Valley fold the left-hand side point over as shown. Repeat behind.

18 Again, treating the points as if they were one, inside reverse fold them upwards, at the same time stretching the folds made in step 17 and making the model become three-dimensional.

19 Once again, treating the points as if they were one, inside reverse fold them towards the left.

20 Inside reverse fold the inner point out towards the right, thereby making a tail fin.

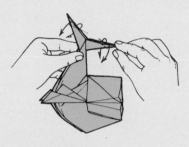

21 Shape the tips of the tail fins with outside reverse folds.

22 Shape the fish's abdomen with a 'soft' mountain fold. Repeat behind. Round out the mouth.

23 Indent the head and tail slightly.

24 Open out the fins, thereby completing the Syachi hoko.

OWL

KENJI JINBO

Try changing the angle of the eyes each time you make this model to see how many different expressions you can give your owl.

USE A SQUARE OF PAPER, WHITE SIDE UP.

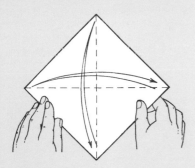

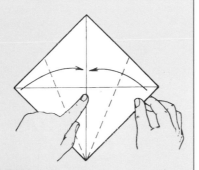

2 From the bottom corner, valley fold the bottom sloping edges over to meet the middle fold-line, thereby making the kite base.

5 Valley fold the bottom left-hand sloping edge up to meet the fold-line made in step 4. Press it flat and unfold it.

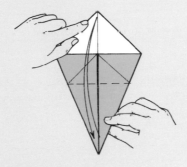

3 Valley fold the kite base in half from bottom to top. Press it flat and unfold it.

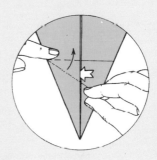

6 Open out the top left-hand layer of paper, . . .

1 Turn the square around to look like a diamond. Valley fold the opposite corners together in turn to mark the diagonal fold-lines, then open up again.

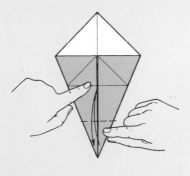

4 Valley fold the bottom point up to meet the fold-line made in step 3. Press it flat and unfold it.

7 at the same time swinging the bottom point over towards the right.

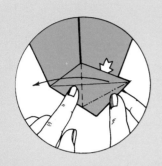

8 Valley fold the point over towards the left along the vertical middle line, at the same time . . .

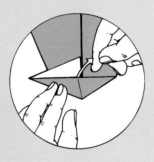

9 letting the paper arrange itself into a sort of petal fold. Press it flat. Pull the inside layer of paper . . .

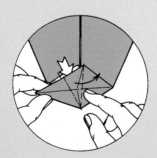

10 out and press it down neatly, thereby making a triangular flap. Open out the flap and squash it down flat.

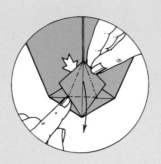

11 Petal fold the squashed flap (see page 124, steps 1 to 6), thereby making the tail.

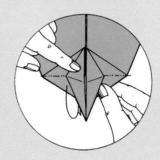

12 Mountain fold the bottom point (which is to be found underneath the tail) behind along the adjacent fold-line.

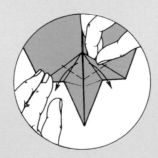

13 Valley fold the two middle points out, thereby making the claws.

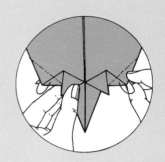

14 Mountain fold behind a little of each side point.

15 This should be the result.

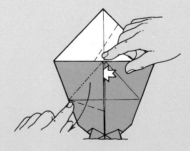

16 On the top left-hand layer of paper, make the valley and mountain folds as shown, thereby opening it out, at the same time . . .

17 taking the left-hand sloping edge over to the right. Press it down neatly.

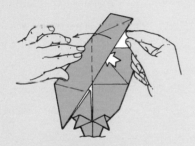

18 Valley fold the top layer of paper over to the left along the middle fold-line, thereby opening it out.

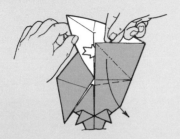

19 Repeat step 16 on the top right-hand layer of paper, at the same time . . .

20 taking the right-hand sloping edge over to the left. Press it down neatly, thereby making a triangular flap.

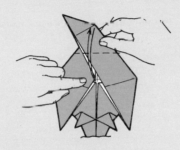

21 Valley fold the flap in half from top to bottom. Press it flat and unfold it.

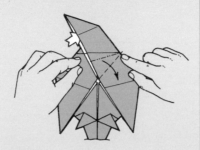

22 On the flap's top layer of paper, make the valley and mountain folds as shown, thereby opening it out.

23 Repeat step 22 on the flap's bottom layer of paper, at the same time flattening the flap down towards you.

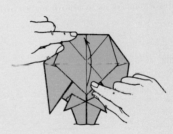

24 Valley fold the flap's bottom point up on a line between the two side points, thereby making a white triangle.

25 Valley fold the triangle's tip down as shown, thereby making the face.

26 Open and squash the face's bottom right-hand corner as shown, and . . .

27 press it down neatly into this position. Repeat steps 26 and 27 with the face's bottom left-hand corner.

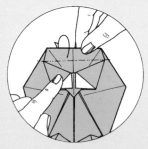

28 Mountain fold the top edge behind.

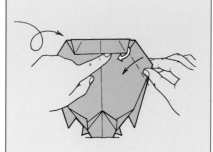

29 Turn the model over. Valley fold the owl's right-hand side over as shown, at the same time rearranging the adjacent layer of paper slightly.

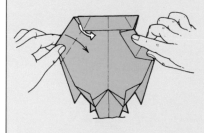

30 With the paper in the same position, repeat step 29 with the owl's left-hand side.

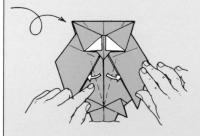

31 Turn the model over. Valley fold the inner edges over as shown.

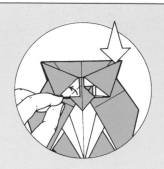

32 Valley fold the face's middle points over a little, thereby suggesting the eyes.

33 Here is the completed owl.

RABBIT

YOSHIHIDE MOMOTANI

This model is a perfect example of how you can use a few folds to create a simple model that suggests the whole form.

USE A RECTANGLE OF PAPER, 2 X 1 IN PROPORTION, WHITE SIDE UP.

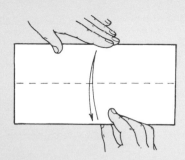

1 Place the rectangle sideways on. Valley fold it in half from bottom to top. Press it flat and unfold it.

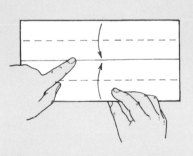

2 Valley fold the top and bottom edges over to meet the middle fold-line.

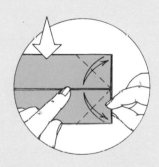

3 Valley fold the top and bottom right-hand corners over to meet the middle edges. Press them flat and unfold them.

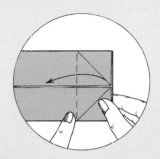

4 Valley fold the right-hand side over as shown, thereby making a flap.

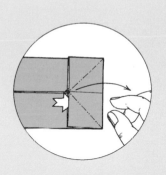

5 Open out the flap's top layer of paper and, . . .

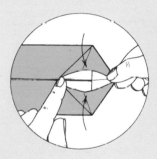

6 along the fold-lines made in step 3, press the paper down neatly into two triangular points.

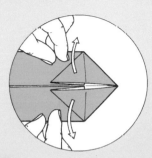

7 Pinch the triangular points and . . .

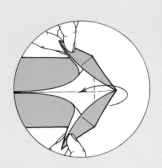

8 stretch them apart, thereby . . .

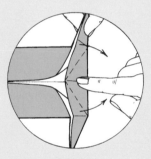

9 flattening down the adjacent side point. Valley fold the top and bottom triangular points over, so . . .

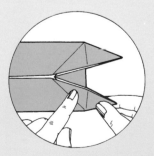

10 they point towards the right. These points will become the rabbit's front paws.

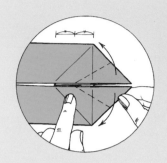

11 Valley fold the right-hand triangular points over as shown.

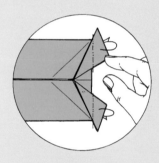

12 Mountain fold the top and bottom right-hand side points behind along the line of the adjacent folded side.

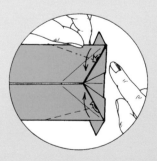

13 Valley fold the hidden top and bottom right-hand corners over on a slant, . . .

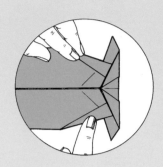

14 at the same time rearranging the adjacent layers of paper.

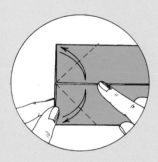

15 Repeat steps 3 to 10 with the top and bottom left-hand corners, making sure that in step 10 they point towards the left. These points will become the rabbit's ears.

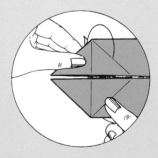

16 Mountain fold the paper in half from top to bottom.

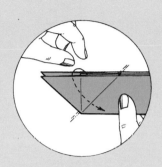

17 Inside reverse fold the 'middle' left-hand layers of paper. The easy way to accomplish this step is to . . .

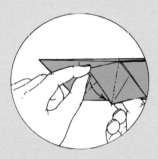

18 take the left-hand triangular point over towards the right as though turning the page of a book, at the same time stretching and flattening down the middle layers of paper.

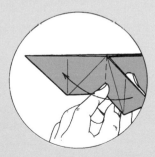

19 Return the triangular point to its original position.

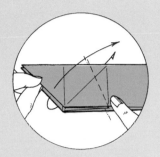

20 Valley fold the top left-hand triangular point over as shown. Repeat behind.

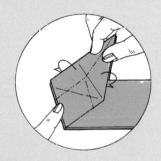

21 Pinch the left-hand point's sloping edges together with a mountain fold.

22 Flatten the point to the left with its edges still pinched together, thereby . . .

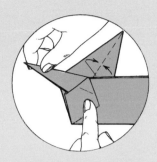

23 performing an origami technique known as a rabbit's ear. Repeat steps 21 to 23 with the remaining left-hand point.

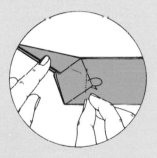

24 Shape the rabbit's chin with a mountain fold. Repeat behind.

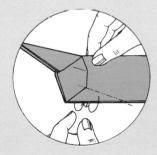

25 Shape the rabbit's neck with a mountain fold. Repeat behind.

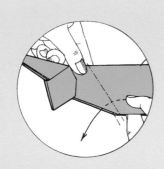

26 Inside reverse fold the right-hand section of paper downwards.

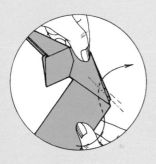

27 Inside reverse fold the section of paper up towards the right, at the same time taking in a little of the rabbit's neck section of paper.

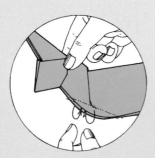

28 Shape the rabbit's chest with a mountain fold. Repeat behind.

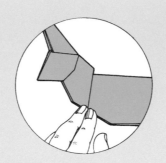

29 This should be the result.

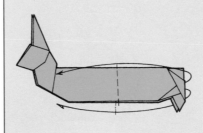

30 Outside reverse fold the right-hand section of paper, at the same time . . .

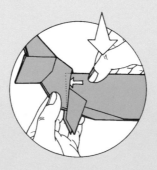

31 inserting the front paws under neath the neck as shown.

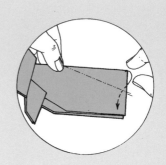

32 Inside reverse fold the top right-hand corner.

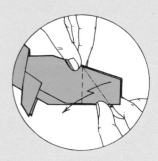

33 Step fold the top right-hand layer of paper, at the same time . . .

34 stretching the top edge down as shown. Press the paper flat.

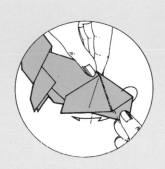

35 Repeat steps 33 and 34 behind. These are the rabbit's back paws.

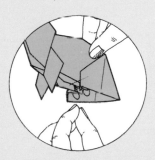

36 The rear flap of each back paw should be refolded inside, thereby locking the body and paws together.

37 Shape the rabbit's tail with a double reverse fold.

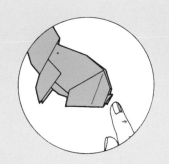

38 This should be the result.

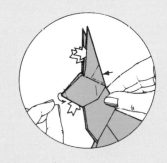

39 Indent the ears and nose slightly, thereby . . .

40 opening them out.

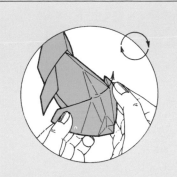

41 Open out the rabbit from underneath, at the same time shaping its back.

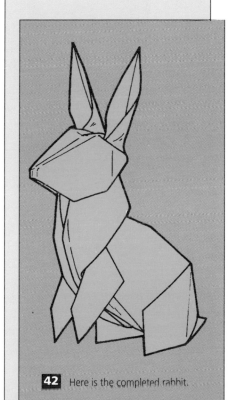

42 Here is the completed rabbit.

CIRCUS ELEPHANT

MEGUMI BIDDLE

Do not be discouraged by the tricky sink folds in steps 18, 19 and 20 of this model, as everything falls into place very easily.

USE AN A-SIZED RECTANGLE OF PAPER, WHITE SIDE UP. YOU WILL ALSO NEED A PAIR OF SCISSORS.

1 Place the rectangle sideways on. Valley fold it in half from bottom to top. Press it flat and unfold it. Cut along the middle fold-line, thereby making two rectangles.

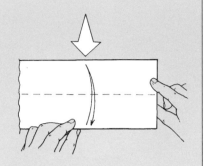

2 Place one rectangle sideways on, with the white side on top. Valley fold it in half from bottom to top. Press it flat and unfold it.

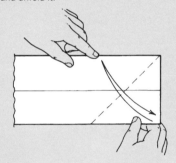

3 Valley fold the right-hand side up to meet the top edge. Press it flat and unfold it.

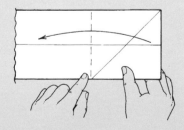

4 Valley fold the right-hand side over as shown, thereby making a flap.

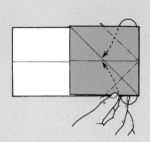

5 Inside reverse fold the top and bottom right-hand corners.

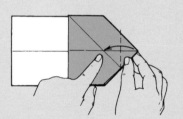

6 Valley fold the right-hand side point over to the intersection of the diagonal and horizontal fold-lines.

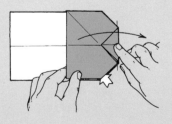

7 Fold the flap of paper over to the right, so that . . .

8 the reversed corners rise up. Squash them down flat into . . .

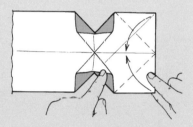

9 this position. Valley fold the top and bottom right-hand corners over to meet the middle fold-line.

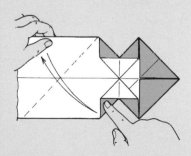

10 Valley fold the left-hand top edge down to the right to lie along the adjacent vertical edges. Press it flat and unfold it.

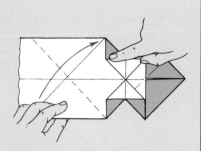

11 Valley fold the left-hand bottom edge up to the right to lie along the adjacent vertical edges.

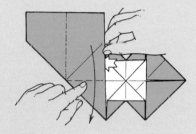

12 Valley fold the left-hand layer of paper down along the middle fold-line, at the same time folding the left-hand side over to lie along the adjacent vertical edges, thereby letting the paper arrange itself in a sort of petal fold (see page 124).

13 Valley fold the left-hand section of paper over to lie along the middle fold-line.

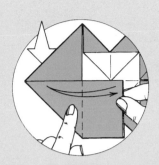

14 Valley fold the rectangular section of paper over as shown. Press it flat and unfold it.

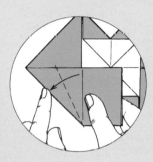

15 Valley fold the rectangular section of paper over, so that the fold-line made in step 14 lies along the adjacent sloping edge.

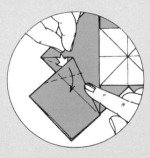

16 Open out and squash down neatly the section of paper's upper point.

17   Press the upper point flat. Unfold the paper back to the beginning of step 13.

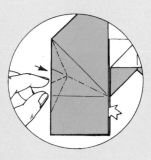

18   Open out the section of paper slightly. Sink the triangular area inwards, as shown by the mountain fold-lines.

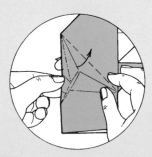

19   Following the existing fold-lines on either side, flatten down . . .

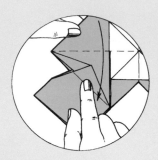

20   the section of paper. Valley fold the main body of paper in half from top to bottom.

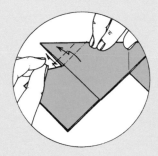

21   Shape the elephant's tail with a double reverse fold, taking two layers of paper to the front and one to the back.

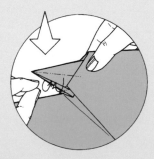

22   Working from the tip, narrow down the tail by mountain folding its edges up inside the model. Press the paper flat (see step 23).

23   This is a view of the tail from inside the model. Note the 'collars' at the base of the tail.

24   Round off the elephant's back with a small sink.

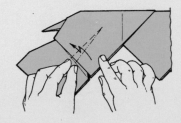

25   Shape the elephant's legs with a step fold. Repeat behind.

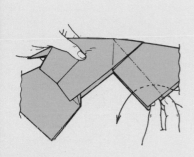

26 Inside reverse fold the top right-hand point down as shown, thereby making the trunk.

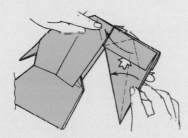

27 Valley fold the trunk's top layer in half, at the same time opening the upper band of paper out and squashing it down towards the elephant's back, thereby making an ear. Repeat behind.

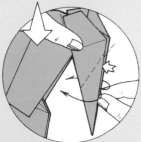

28 Outside reverse fold the trunk.

29 Again, outside reverse fold the trunk.

30 Inside reverse fold the trunk's tip. Shape the ear with a step fold. Repeat behind.

31 Shape the front leg with a mountain fold. Repeat behind.

32 Mountain fold the right-hand side of the elephant's platform into the model. Repeat behind.

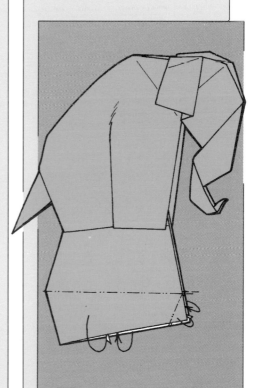

33 Shape the platform by mountain folding its bottom edges and right-hand corners up inside the model, thereby completing the circus elephant.

KOALA

YOSHIHIDE MOMOTANI

Try to find the best colour and texture of paper for this model, as it will enhance the finished item and make it look more realistic.

USE A SQUARE OF PAPER, WHITE SIDE UP.

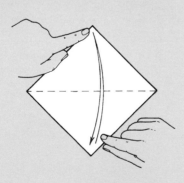

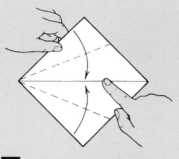

2 From the left-hand corner, valley fold the top and bottom sloping edges over to meet the middle fold-line, thereby making the kite base.

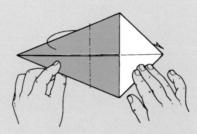

3 Mountain fold the kite base in half from left to right.

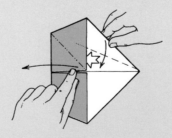

4 Pull the top flap of paper over . . .

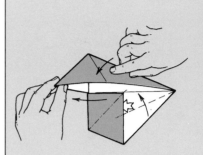

5 to the left, so its sloping edge comes to rest along the middle fold-line. Press the paper flat, to make a triangular point. Repeat steps 4 and 5 with the bottom flap of paper, thereby . . .

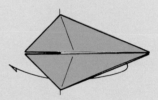

6 making a shape that in origami is called the fish base. Valley fold the underneath right-hand point over to the left on a line between the top and bottom points, thereby making a fish base in it's 'opened' form.

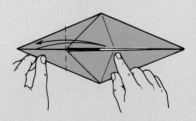

7 Valley fold the left-hand side point over as shown. Press it flat and unfold it.

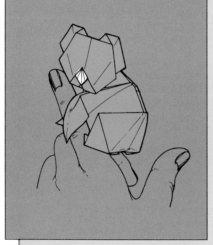

1 Turn the square around to look like a diamond. Valley fold it in half from bottom to top. Press it flat and unfold it.

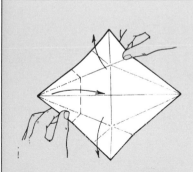

8 Open out the fish base, with the white side on top. Valley fold the left-hand side point over along the fold-line made in step 7, at the same time . . .

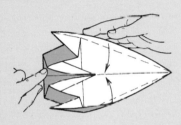

9 reforming the fish base along the existing fold-lines, as shown.

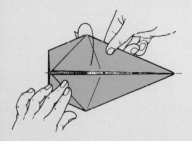

10 Mountain fold the top behind to the bottom.

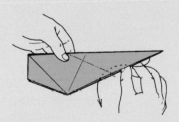

11 Inside reverse fold the right-hand point downwards.

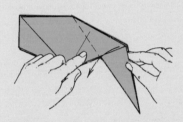

12 Valley fold the reversed point's top layer of paper over to the left.

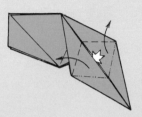

13 Open out the reversed point, at the same time . . .

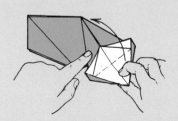

14 lifting its bottom point upwards, thereby making the koala's face and head.

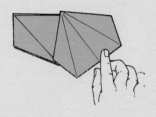

15 Press the paper flat into this position.

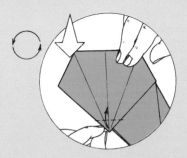

16 Turn the model around, into the position shown. Valley fold the face's bottom point up, thereby making a small white triangle. This is the koala's nose.

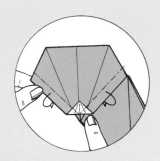

17 Mountain fold the face's lower sloping edges behind as shown, thereby making the nose become diamond-like in shape.

18 Valley fold the nose up along a horizontal line that runs adjacent to its top point.

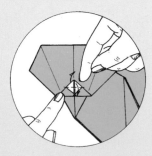

19 Valley fold the nose in half from top to bottom, at the same time letting the paper from underneath flick up.

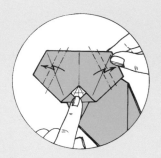

20 Shape the ears with step folds as shown.

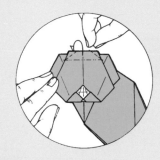

21 Shape the head with a mountain fold between the ears, at the same time . . .

22 taking in just a little of the paper that forms the ears, as shown. Valley fold the triangular pointed flap over. Repeat behind.

23 Valley fold the triangular pointed flap over along it's upper edge. Repeat behind. These are the koala's front paws.

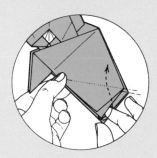

24 Inside reverse fold the 'middle' right-hand layers of paper, thereby making two flaps of paper.

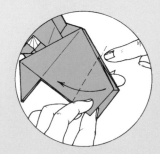

25 Valley fold the right-hand flap of paper over. Repeat behind. These are the koala's back paws.

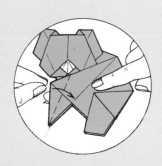

26 Valley fold the front paw's short sloping edge over to lie along the adjacent fold-line. Repeat behind.

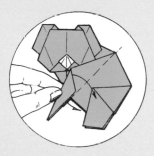

27 Valley fold the front paw over along the adjacent fold-line. Repeat behind.

28 Open out the front paw slightly, thereby making the valley fold as shown. Repeat behind.

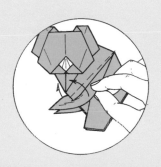

29 Valley fold the front paw up underneath the face, at the same time letting it swing around into the position shown in step 30. Repeat behind.

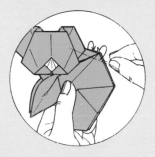

30 Shape the back with a mountain fold, thereby locking the front paw into place. Repeat behind.

31 Shape the back paw with a mountain fold. Repeat behind.

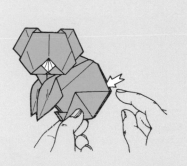

32 Make the koala become three-dimensional by opening out its inside ridge of paper.

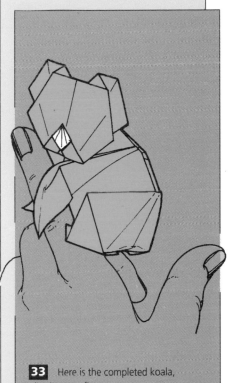

33 Here is the completed koala, clinging to a finger.

RHINOCEROS

EDWIN CORRIE

This model is one of many that Edwin Corrie has created from an A-sized rectangle of paper. With this piece of origami, try to make your folds as neat, tidy and accurate as possible.

USE AN A-SIZED RECTANGLE OF PAPER, COLOURED ON BOTH SIDES.

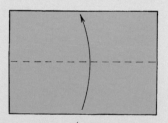

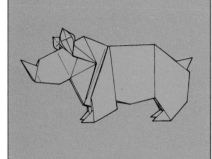

1 Place the rectangle sideways on. Valley fold it in half from bottom to top.

2 Valley fold the paper as shown. Press the folds flat and unfold them.

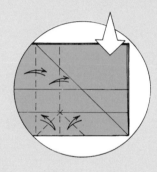

3 Again, valley fold the paper as shown. Press the folds flat and unfold them.

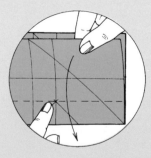

4 Valley fold the top layer of paper down along the lower horizontal fold-line made in step 2.

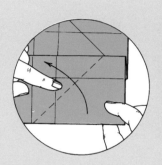

5 Valley fold the bottom edge up along the diagonal fold-line made in step 2, making . . .

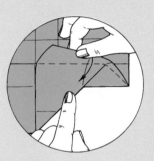

6 the adjacent side rise up. Flatten the side down, thereby making a band of paper.

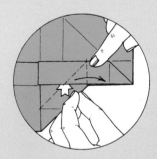

7 Open out the band of paper and squash it down neatly, into the position shown in step 8.

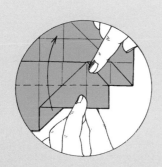

8 Valley fold the bottom edge up along the adjacent horizontal fold-line.

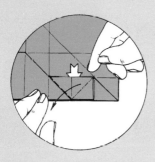

9 Open out the top layer of paper and squash it down neatly, into the position shown in step 10, thereby . . .

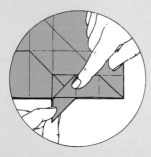

10 making an ear.

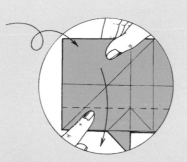

11 Turn the paper over from right to left. Repeat steps 4 to 10.

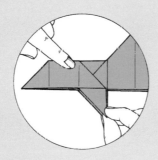

12 This should be the result.

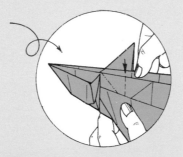

13 Turn the paper over from bottom to top. Open out the paper slightly and, along the existing fold-lines, flatten the middle folded ridge of paper out.

14 Push the middle ridge of paper down, as shown by the valley fold-lines.

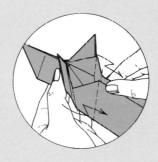

15 On either side, step fold the paper, thereby flattening it down neatly, into the position shown in step 16.

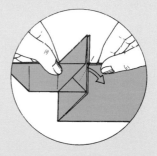

16 Hold the paper where shown and carefully swivel the ears apart from the main body of paper.

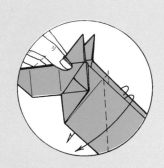

17 Outside reverse fold.

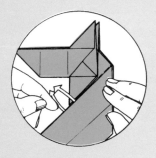

18 Carefully pull out one layer of paper on each side.

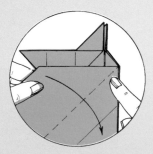

19 Valley fold the front layer in half from side to side. Repeat behind.

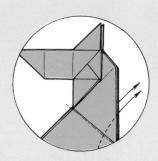

20 Double inside reverse fold. The model will need to be opened out for this step to take place.

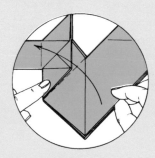

21 Valley fold the front layer over.

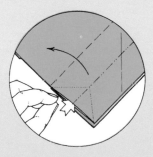

22 Lift the middle layer up, . . .

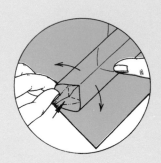

23 open it out and squash it down symmetrically.

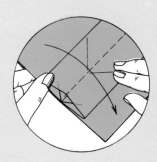

24 This should be the result. Valley fold the layers back.

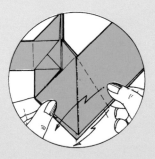

25 Shape the front legs symmetrically with step folds.

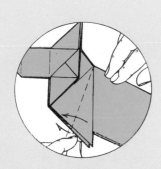

26 Shape the front leg with a valley fold. Repeat behind.

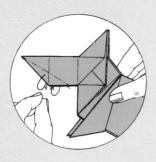

27 Shape the horn with a mountain fold. Repeat behind.

28 Double reverse fold the horn.

29 Valley fold the ears over towards the horn.

30 Open out one ear and squash it down neatly.

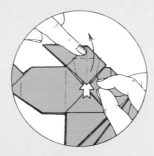

31 Pinch and lift up the ear's front flap of paper, thereby . . .

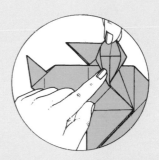

32 letting the paper arrange itself in a sort of petal fold (see page 124). Repeat steps 30 to 32 with the remaining ear.

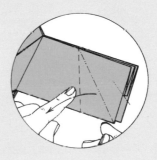

33 Step fold the top right-hand layer of paper, at the same time . . .

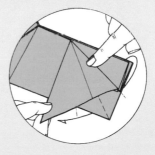

34 stretching the top edge down as shown. Press the paper flat. Repeat steps 33 and 34 behind.

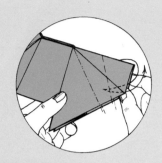

35 Double reverse fold the top right-hand point, thereby making the tail.

36 Shape the tail by repeating steps 22 and 23 of the circus elephant on page 158.

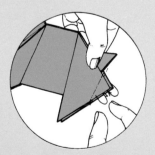

37 Shape the back leg with a mountain fold. Repeat behind.

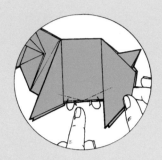

38 Shape the abdomen with mountain folds, thereby forming squash folds on the inside. Repeat behind.

39 This is a view of the model from the underneath, showing the result of step 38.

40 Shape the front leg with a double reverse fold. Repeat behind.

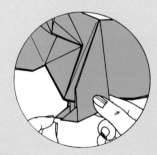

41 This should be the result. Repeat step 40 with the back legs.

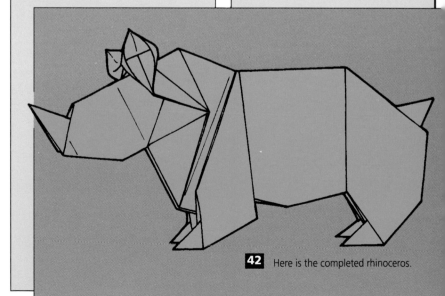

42 Here is the completed rhinoceros.

CELEBRATED EXTINCT ANIMALS

In the following pages, you will learn how to fold some of the world's most distinguished extinct animals. They range from a simple dinosaur to a difficult pteranodon (with all its claws).

Dinosaurs are among the most demanding subjects to fold in the world of origami. A few of the models may appear daunting at first, but they are actually very easy to fold. Remember, as with any model, to fold neatly and look very carefully at each illustration to see what you should do.

SIMPLE DINOSAUR

RACHEL KATZ

This is the perfect model to teach a young child.

USE A RECTANGLE OF PAPER, A4 IN SIZE, WHITE SIDE UP. YOU WILL ALSO NEED A PAIR OF SCISSORS.

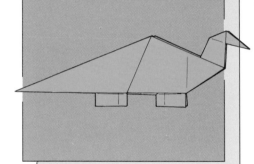

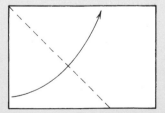

1 Place the rectangle sideways on. Valley fold the left-hand side up to meet the top, thereby making a triangle.

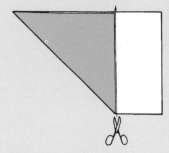

2 Cut along the side of the triangle. Save the rectangular piece of paper for the dinosaur's legs. Open out the triangle into a square.

Body

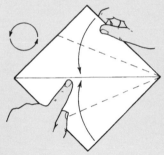

3 With the white side on top, turn the square around to look like a diamond, making sure the existing fold-line is running horizontally across the paper. From the right-hand corner, valley fold the top and bottom sloping edges over to meet the middle fold-line, thereby making the kite base.

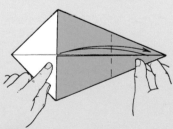

4 Valley fold the right-hand point over to meet the vertical edges. Press it flat and unfold it.

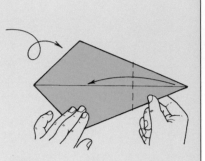

5 Turn the paper over. Valley fold the right-hand point over along the fold-line made in step 4.

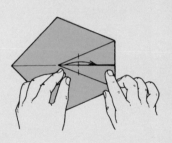

6 Valley fold the point back out towards the right.

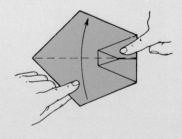

7 Valley fold the paper in half from bottom to top.

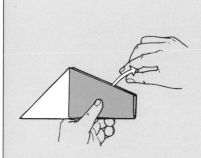

8 Reach inside the model and pull out the . . .

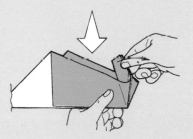

9 dinosaur's neck. Press it flat, into the position shown in step 10.

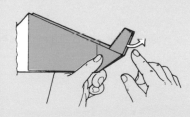

10 Reach inside the neck and pull out the . . .

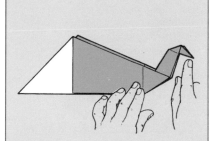

11 head. Press it flat, into the position shown, thereby completing the body.

Legs

12 Place the rectangular piece of paper sideways on, with the white side on top. Valley fold it in half from bottom to top. Press the paper flat and unfold it.

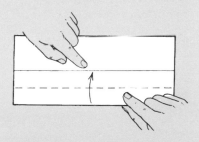

13 Valley fold the bottom edge up to meet the middle fold-line.

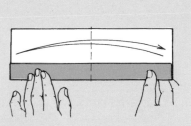

14 Valley fold the paper in half from side to side. Press it flat and unfold it.

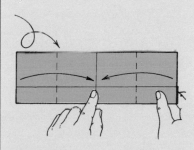

15 Turn the paper over. Valley fold the sides over to meet the middle fold-line.

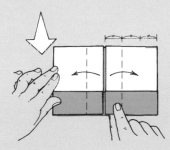

16 Valley fold the centre edges out to points one-third of the distance to their adjacent sides, thereby making two bands of paper.

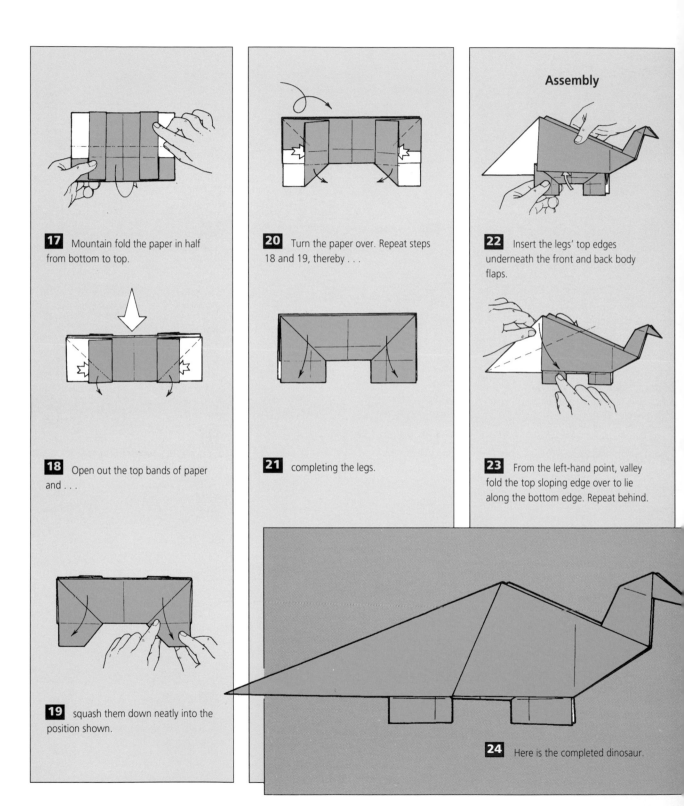

17   Mountain fold the paper in half from bottom to top.

18   Open out the top bands of paper and . . .

19   squash them down neatly into the position shown.

20   Turn the paper over. Repeat steps 18 and 19, thereby . . .

21   completing the legs.

Assembly

22   Insert the legs' top edges underneath the front and back body flaps.

23   From the left-hand point, valley fold the top sloping edge over to lie along the bottom edge. Repeat behind.

24   Here is the completed dinosaur.

TYRANNOSAURUS

M E G U M I   B I D D L E

When two different pieces of origami are joined together to make one model, the result is called compound origami. This technique is very useful for making animals, as you can fold the front half from one square and the rear half from another.

USE TWO SQUARES OF PAPER, ONE THREE-QUARTERS THE SIZE OF THE OTHER, BOTH WHITE SIDE UP. YOU WILL ALSO NEED A TUBE OF PAPER GLUE.

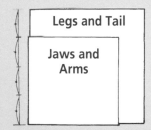

Make sure the sides of the smaller square are three-quarters the length of the sides of the larger square. For example, if the large piece of paper is 30 cm (12 inches) square, the smaller piece should be 23 cm (9 inches) square.

Legs and Tail

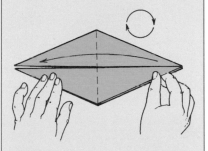

1   Fold the larger square into a bird base (see pages 124 to 125, steps 1 to 8). Turn the base around so that its flaps point to the right. Valley fold the front flap over towards the left.

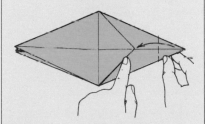

2   Valley fold the back flap's tip over to meet the adjacent point.

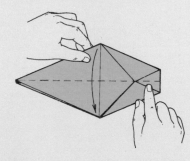

3   Valley fold the paper in half from top to bottom.

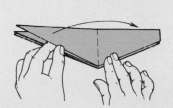

4   Valley fold the front left-hand flap across to the other side.

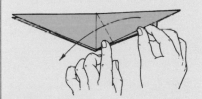

5   Valley fold the flap down as shown, thereby . . .

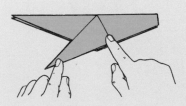

6   making a leg.

7   Outside reverse fold the leg.

8   Shape the thigh with an inside reverse fold. Shape the leg with outside and inside reverse folds.

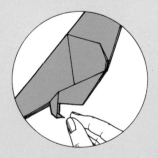

9   This should be the result.

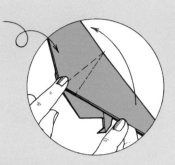

10   Turn the model over. Valley fold the lower front flap over as shown, thereby making another leg. Repeat steps 7 and 8.

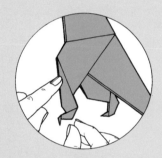

11   Arrange the legs so that one is in front of the other.

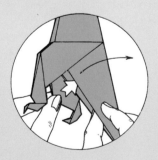

12   Open out the middle point.

13   This is a view of the model from the inside. Valley fold the middle point's sloping sides over a little.

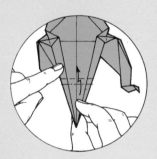

14   Step fold the middle point as shown.

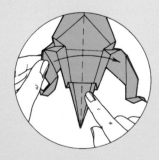

15   Valley fold the middle point in half from left to right.

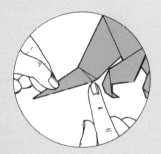

16 Pull up the middle point as far . . .

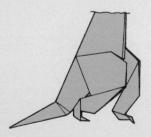

17 as the hidden step fold will allow you, thereby making the tail.

18 Here are the completed legs and tail.

Jaws and Arms

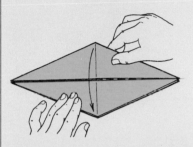

19 Fold the smaller square into a bird base (see page 124 to 125, steps 1 to 8). Turn the base around so that its flaps point to the right. Valley fold the base in half from top to bottom.

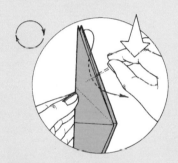

20 Turn the paper around, so that its right-hand point becomes the top. Inside reverse fold the inner flap, thereby making the lower jaw.

21 Mountain fold the jaw's top points down inside the jaw.

22 Inside reverse fold the outer flap, thereby making the upper jaw.

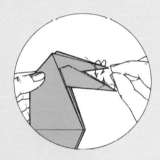

23 Outside reverse fold the upper jaw's tip. Inside reverse fold the lower jaw's tip.

24 Valley fold the front bottom flap over to lie along the adjacent horizontal fold-line, thereby making an arm.

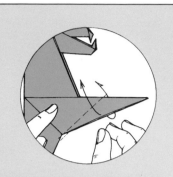

25 Outside reverse fold the arm.

26 Shape the arm with an outside reverse fold.

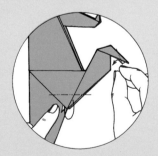

27 Shape the arm's tip with an inside reverse fold. Mountain fold the arm's bottom point behind.

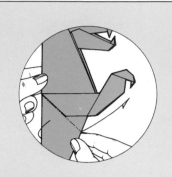

28 Repeat steps 24 to 27 behind with the remaining bottom flap.

29 To complete, arrange the arms so that one is in front of the other.

Assembly

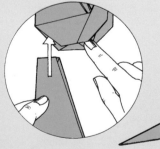

30 Insert the legs and tail between the arms as shown.

31 This is a view of the model from the inside. Note the position of the two pieces. Glue them together.

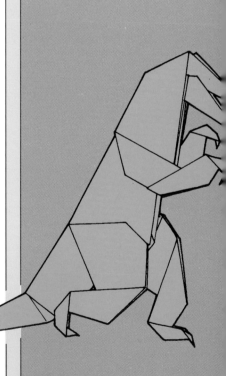

32 Here is the completed tyrannosaurus.

APATOSAURUS

STEVE BIDDLE

One is not restricted to folding models from one particular base alone, as it is sometimes possible to combine two bases. This model is made from a combination of the blintz and fish bases.

USE A SQUARE OF PAPER, WHITE SIDE UP.

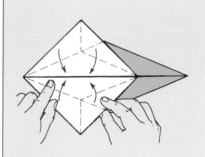

2 Mountain fold the left-hand corners and valley fold the right-hand corners into the middle, thereby making a sort of blintz base.

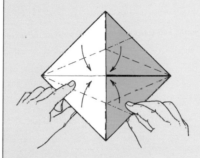

3 Pinch the bottom point's sloping sides together with a valley fold. Flatten the point to the right with it's sides still pinched together. Repeat this step with the top point, thereby . . .

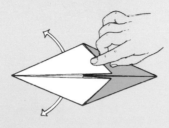

4 making a fish base in it's 'opened' form (see page 160). Bring out the left-hand corners from behind the base.

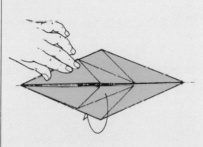

5 Repeat step 3 with the left hand corners, thereby making another 'opened' fish base.

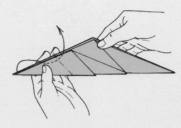

6 Mountain fold the paper in half from bottom to top.

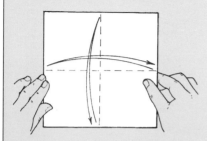

7 Inside reverse fold the left-hand point upwards, thereby making the neck.

1 Valley fold the opposite sides and top and bottom edges together in turn to mark the vertical and horizontal fold-lines, then open up again.

8 Starting from the tip, valley fold the top layer of the neck in half, at the same time inside reverse folding the triangular area, as shown. Repeat behind.

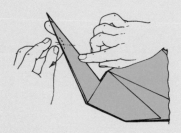

9 Inside reverse fold the neck, thereby making the head.

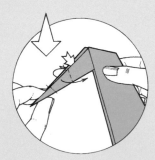

10 Shape the lower jaw with a double outside reverse fold.

11 This should be the result.

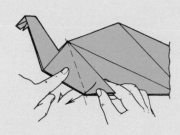

12 Valley fold the left-hand triangular flap over, thereby making a front leg. Repeat behind.

13 Shape the front leg with a double reverse fold. Repeat behind.

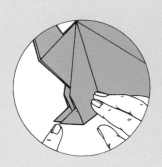

14 This should be the result.

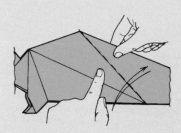

15 Valley fold the right-hand point over along the sloping edge of the adjacent triangular flap. Press it flat and unfold it.

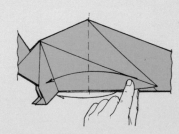

16 Valley fold the right-hand triangular flap over towards the left. Repeat behind. These are the back legs.

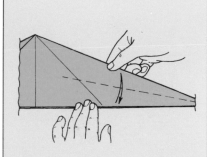

17 Valley fold the right-hand point in half from bottom to top. Press down on the paper only from the point's tip to the sloping fold-line made in step 15, then unfold it.

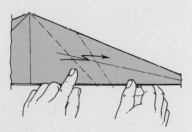

18 Along the fold-line made in step 15, step fold the right-hand point.

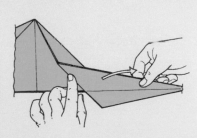

19 Press the step fold flat, and then unfold it.

20 Along the existing fold-lines, double reverse fold the right-hand point. The model . . .

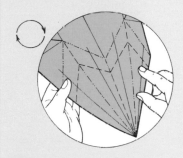

21 will need to be opened out for this step to take place.

22 Flatten the paper down neatly, into the position shown in step 23.

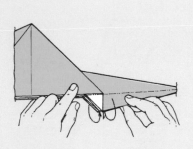

23 Mountain fold the right-hand point's front layer of paper up inside the model. Repeat behind.

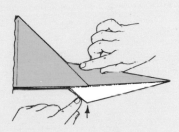

24 Sink the right-hand point's middle section of paper. The model . . .

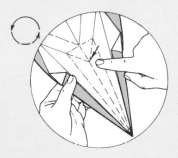

25 will need to be opened out for this step to take place.

26 Flatten the paper down neatly into the position shown in step 27.

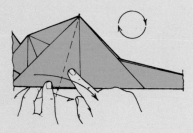

27 Valley fold the back leg over towards the right. Repeat behind.

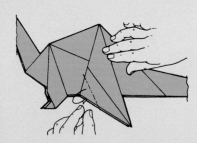

28 Shape the thigh with a mountain fold. Repeat behind.

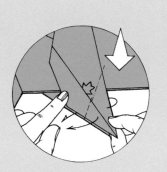

29 Outside reverse fold the back leg, arranging the paper into the position shown in step 30.

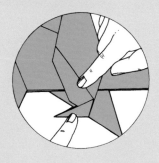

30 This should be the result. Repeat step 29 behind.

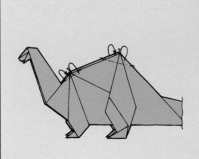

31 Round off the back with mountain folds. Repeat behind.

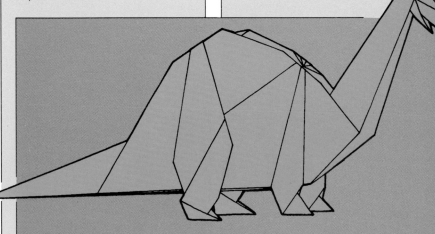

32 Here is the completed apatosaurus.

PTERANODON

FUMIAKI KAWABATA

This is a very challenging piece of origami, and is best not attempted until you have a good understanding of the various origami procedures and techniques.

As always, follow the illustrations very carefully.

USE A LARGE SQUARE OF THIN, BUT STRONG PAPER, WHITE SIDE UP.

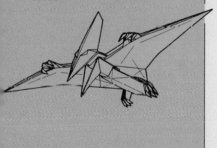

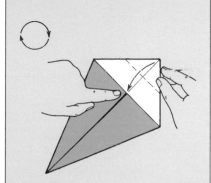

1 Begin with a kite base (see page 36, steps 18 and 19). Valley fold the top point down to meet the adjacent edges, thereby . . .

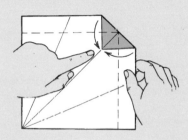

2 making a triangle. Unfold the top and bottom flaps of paper.

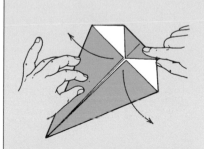

3 Valley fold the top edge and right-hand side over as shown, thereby making two bands of paper.

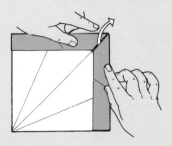

4 Release the triangle from underneath the bands of paper, thereby making a triangular flap.

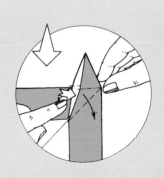

5 Open out the flap and squash it down neatly . . .

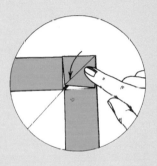

6 into a preliminary fold.

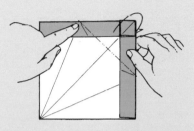

7 Mountain fold the preliminary fold behind along the line where the sloping fold-lines intersect with the top edge and right-hand side.

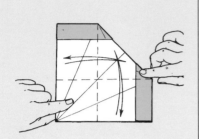

8 Valley fold the bottom edge and the left-hand side over as shown. Press them flat and unfold them.

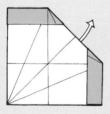

9 Bring out the preliminary fold from behind.

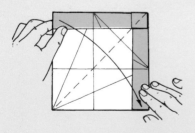

10 Valley fold the paper in half from top left to bottom right.

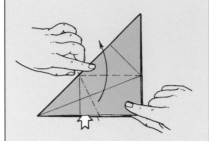

11 Open out the bottom section of paper, squashing it down neatly, into the position shown in step 12, thereby making a flap.

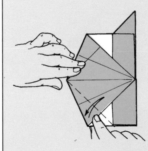

12 Along the existing fold-line, valley fold the flap's bottom sloping edge over. Press it flat and unfold it.

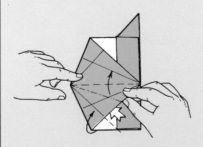

13 Along the existing horizontal fold-line, open out the flap's lower section of paper and . . .

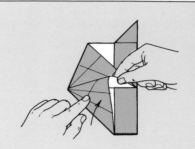

14 squash it down neatly as shown.

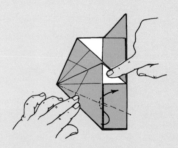

15 Inside reverse fold the flap's bottom section of paper, thereby making a diamond-like shape.

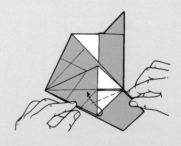

16 Inside reverse fold the diamond's bottom corner as shown.

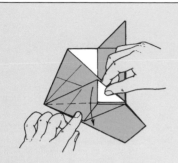

17 Valley fold the diamond-like shape in half from top to bottom.

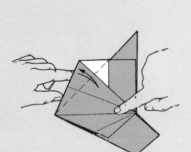

18 Repeat step 12 with the flap's top sloping edge.

19 Repeat steps 13 to 17 with the flap's upper section of paper.

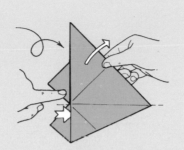

20 Turn the model over. Pull the triangular flap over towards the right, thereby rearranging the bottom layers of paper.

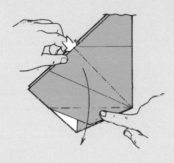

21 Open out the triangular flap, squashing it down neatly, into the position shown in step 22.

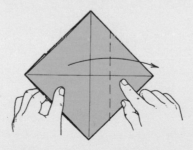

22 As far as possible, valley fold the left-hand layers of paper over to the right.

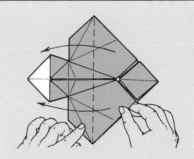

23 Valley fold the right-hand flaps of paper over to the left on a line between the top and bottom points.

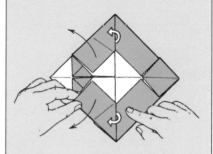

24 Pull out the left-hand bands of paper, releasing them from underneath the vertical folded edge, thereby making two flaps.

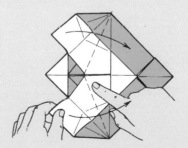

25 Valley fold the flaps over to the right as shown.

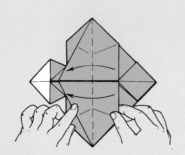

26 Valley fold the flaps over towards the left on a line between the top and bottom points.

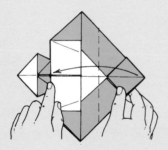

27 Valley fold the right-hand point over to meet the flap's left-hand side, thereby making a triangle.

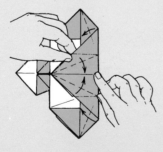

28 Working from its tip, bring the triangle's (but not the preliminary fold's) sloping edges together along the middle fold-line, pressing the base of the triangle into collars.

29 Insert the collars into the model (but in front of the underneath section of paper) with a mountain fold, at the same time . . .

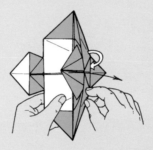

30 letting the preliminary fold swing across to the right.

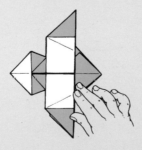

31 This should be the result. Press the paper flat.

32 Valley fold the upper flap's bottom right-hand corner over as shown. Press it flat and unfold it.

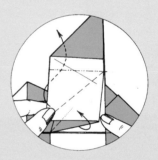

33 Along the fold-line made in step 32, inside reverse fold the upper flap's front layer of paper, at the same time . . .

34 swinging its bottom left-hand corner into the position shown. Press the paper down neatly, thereby . . .

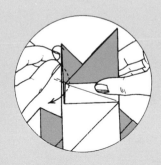

35 making a triangular point. Inside reverse fold the point, so that its sloping ridge lies along the adjacent horizontal edge.

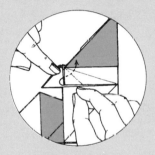

36 Inside reverse fold the triangular point's adjacent corner.

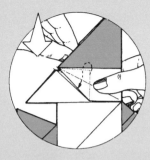

37 Again, inside reverse fold the corner. The upper flap will need to be opened out for this step to take place.

38 As far as possible, valley fold the upper flap's front sloping edge over.

39 Inside reverse fold the triangular point.

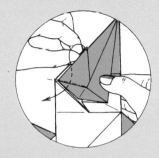

40 Again, inside reverse fold the triangular point.

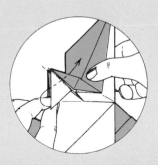

41 Once again, inside reverse fold the triangular point.

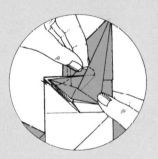

42 Finally, inside reverse fold the triangular point as shown.

43 Form one set of front claws with inside reverse folds.

44 Valley fold the front claws up.

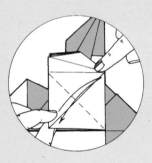

45 Valley fold one of the upper flap's bottom edges over as shown. Press it flat and unfold it.

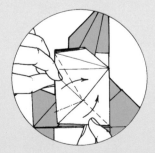

46 Along the fold-line made in step 45, refold the bottom edge, at the same time . . .

47 pushing the flap's side across. Press the paper down neatly into the position shown in step 48.

48 Valley fold the front claws down.

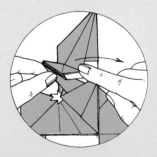

49 Valley fold the claws over to the right.

50 Valley fold the claws over, so that the adjoining sloping edge lies along the adjacent fold-line.

51 Mountain fold the claws behind as shown, inserting . . .

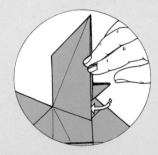

52 them into the model and in the process making a wing. Repeat steps 32 to 52 with the lower flap, thereby making . . .

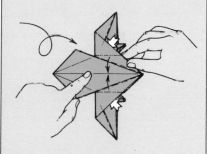

53 another set of front claws and a wing.

54 Turn the model over from top to bottom. Working from the right-hand side point, bring the top and bottom sloping edges together along the middle fold-line, pressing them . . .

55 down neatly into collars.

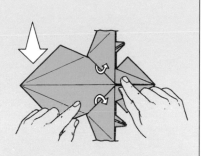

56 Release the flap from . . .

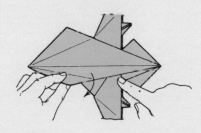

57 underneath the collars.

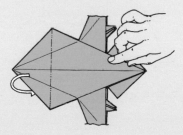

58 Insert the flap's left-hand side point into the model with a mountain fold as shown.

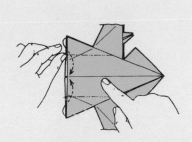

59 Inside reverse fold the flap's top and bottom left-hand points.

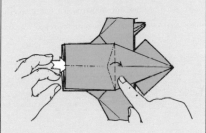

60 On the front flap of paper, make the mountain and valley folds as shown, thereby . . .

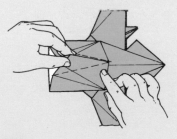

61 bringing the top and bottom left-hand horizontal edges together.

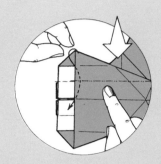

62 Press the paper down, thereby making a triangular flap.

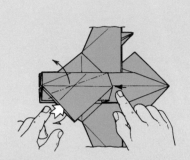

65 Open out the triangular flap, at the same time . . .

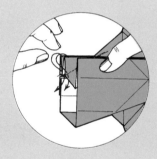

68 Inside reverse fold the flap's top sloping edge along the line of the horizontal edge behind.

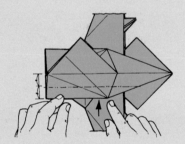

63 Sink the bottom horizontal edge into the model as far as shown.

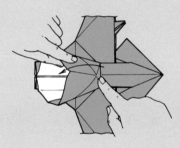

66 flattening out its top point. Squash the flap down neatly . . .

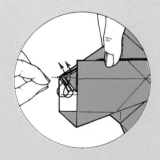

69 Inside reverse fold the flap's left-hand corners as shown.

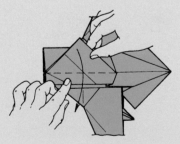

64 Valley fold the triangular flap down along the middle fold-line. Repeat step 63 with the top horizontal edge.

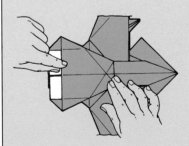

67 into the position shown.

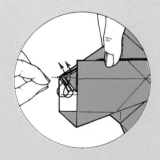

70 Again, inside reverse fold the corners.

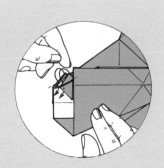

71 Once again, inside reverse fold the corners.

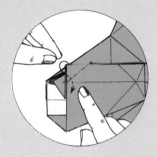

72 Inside reverse fold the flap's middle point as shown.

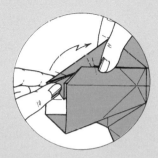

73 Swing the reversed corners towards the opposite side, by step folding. Press them down neatly into the position shown in step 74.

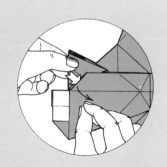

74 Open out the paper slightly.

75 Make the valley and mountain folds as shown.

76 Press the paper down neatly, thereby forming one set of back claws.

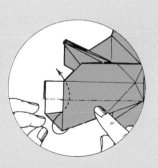

77 Repeat steps 68 to 76 with the flap's bottom sloping edge, thereby making another set of back claws.

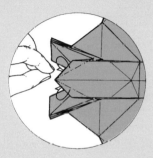

78 Shape the tail with mountain folds.

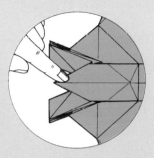

79 This should be the result.

80 Turn the model over from top to bottom. Inside reverse fold the topmost layer of each set of back claws.

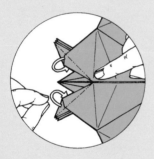

81 Mountain fold the topmost layer of each set of back claws behind, at the same time . . .

82 inserting it in front of the adjacent layer of paper.

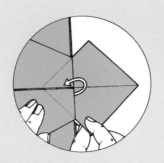

83 Release the preliminary fold's front flap of paper.

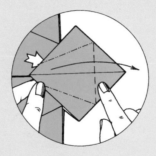

84 Pinch and lift up the preliminary fold's front flap of paper. Take it over to the right, petal folding it as shown.

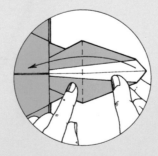

85 Valley fold the petal fold in half from right to left, thereby making the head.

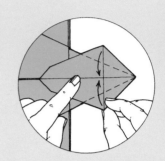

86 Working from the right-hand side point, valley fold the top and bottom sloping edges over to lie along the middle fold-line.

87 Shape the eyes with valley folds.

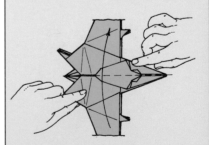

88 Valley fold the model in half from bottom to top.

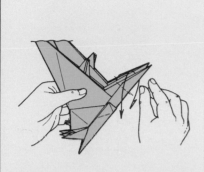

89 Outside reverse fold the topmost folded point downwards, thereby making the lower jaw.

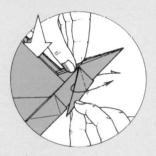

90 Shape the lower jaw with an outside reverse fold.

91 Shape the top jaw with an outside reverse fold, at the same time . . .

92 letting the head and eyes swing up into place.

93 Shape each claw with . . .

94 an outside reverse fold.

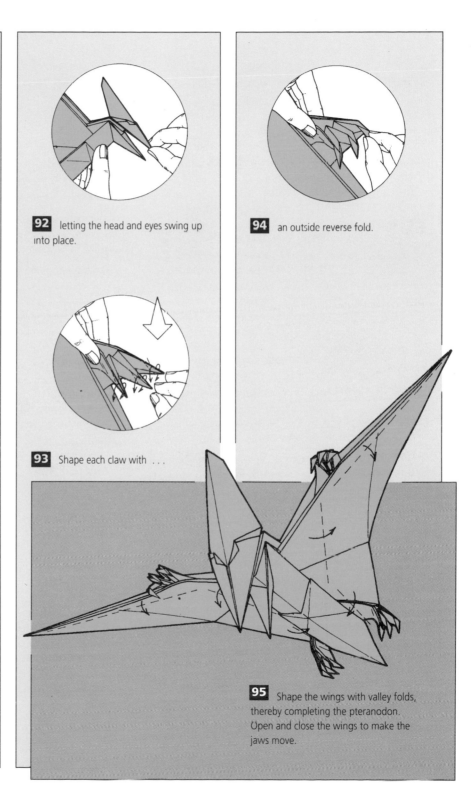

95 Shape the wings with valley folds, thereby completing the pteranodon. Open and close the wings to make the jaws move.

Index